GRIEF MINISTRY

Revised Edition

Terence P. Curley

LITURGICAL PRESS
Collegeville, Minnesota

www.litpress.org

1	2	3	4	5	6	7	8	9

Library of Congress Control Number: 2015950489

ISBN 978-0-8146-4657-1   ISBN 978-0-8146-4681-6 (ebook)

In loving memory of my older brother
Edmund C. Curley,
"my first editor"

Contents

Preface

Grief Ministry is an updated and revised version of *The Ministry of Consolers.* Psychological theories about grief have changed. Most notable is the change in understanding about the bonds we have with loved ones. Rather than disengaging ("letting go"), now becoming prevalent is the understanding about our relationship in psychological terms of having a continual or enduring bond ("connecting") with those who have died. This is not new to Catholic belief as we have always maintained our belief in the communion of saints and praying for those who have gone before us in faith. The new psychology is far more compatible with Catholic belief. It assists us to communicate deep meaning and comfort while we minister to the bereaved.

Grief Ministry focuses us on certain descriptions for ministering to the bereaved. It intends to assist us in finding our place in the ministry of consolation. This book is for those who are ministering and also for the bereaved, families, hospitals, and hospice care. Insights are provided along with each chapter highlighting a "ministry toolbox" as an aid.

May the peace of the Lord be with you as you give of yourselves and your hopes to those who are grieving.

1

Grief Ministry and Those Who Minister

The Spirit of the Lord GOD is upon me,
because the LORD has anointed me;
he has sent me to bring good news to the oppressed, . . .
to comfort all who mourn; . . .
to give them a garland instead of ashes,
the oil of gladness instead of mourning. (Isa 61:1-3)

All ministry requires formation. It must never be taken for granted or done in a cursory way. Ministry is the very life of the church. In, with, and through Christ, we minister to one another. Our words and actions bear fruit in the way we minister in Christ's name and the name of the church. We continually ask our loving God to bring to fruition in our ministries the good work begun in our baptism.

As Christians we are familiar with St. Paul's emphasis on many ministries. When we consider the ministry of consolation we turn to Paul and his communal observation: "If one member [of the Body of Christ, which is the church,] suffers, all suffer together" (1 Cor 12:26). When we explore grief ministry and its many aspects being lived out in community, we really experience what it means to console one another.

Ministry and Community

We are members of the believing community and are responsible for mission and ministry. Our ministry and participation is rooted in the "hope that comes from faith in the saving death and resurrection of the Lord Jesus Christ."[1] In imitation of Jesus we need to seek formation for the community to effectively minister. We must recall that Jesus surrounded himself with disciples and sent them forth two by two to bring the Good News of salvation. When we minister in the ministry of consolation it is best to keep in mind that what we do is done as a representative of the believing community. A collaborative approach to ministry is essential for the ministry to be lasting. It is also essential for one who ministers to be in collaboration with others not only for support but for ongoing formation.

When grief ministry is collaborative and community based, it can very rewarding. This may seem like a different kind of remark to make especially about the ministry that intervenes with those who are deeply suffering the loss of a loved one. After three decades of ministering to the bereaved, I am still amazed at this ministry. The encounter with the infinite is immediate and pervasive. As such, these are graced moments in abundance for all involved. When the bereaved receive support and consolation transformations are almost instantly apparent. This is not always clear in other ministries.

Our rewards are immediate when we witness acceptance and relief by the bereaved as they trust us and relate their story of loss. In every parish there are those who are suffering the loss of a loved one. We need to reach out to them and gently help them realize that eventually their loving God will turn their darkness into light. In this ministry we have an important role to play in the way people go through the process of grieving.

Within the ministry of consolation there are a number of ways that focus on particular aspects of grieving. One could minister as a home visitor, liturgical helper, family support person, support group facilitator, funeral follow-up visitor, hospice care provider, and more. Some of these consoling ministries require more formation than others. All require ongoing ways to come together with other grief ministers and join in prayer, reflection, and discussion (in accordance with confidences that must be kept).[2] It is necessary for the minister not only to identify for the bereaved a support network but also to choose ways to minister. This requires knowledge about how ministry is practiced.

Finding Your Place in Ministry

The grief minister enters into a covenant for caring with the parish. A covenant means that there is a bond between the parties. There are important considerations as we accept the call to minister. Some of the following may help in discerning how to find your place in this ministry.

1. *Prayer/reflection:* Prepare through prayer what you believe God is asking. Are you willing to pray in response to what you feel God is asking you to do?

2. *Establish relationships inside the bereavement ministry:* Are you ready and able to find your voice in bereavement ministry?

3. *Personal history issues addressed:* Have you examined your personal "loss history" and how it will impact what you do?

4. *Discernment with pastoral staff:* Are you ready to ask the pastoral staff for approval and support for the ministry?

5. *Formation and support:* Have you identified how you will be supported and grow in this ministry?

6. *Availability and dedication:* Are there situations where you would feel it difficult to minister?

7. *New approaches:* Are you aware of new approaches and new psychology for loss?

8. *Role in ministry:* Do you understand your role in ministry as helping the bereaved to reconstruct meaning and hope in their lives, not to sever all bonds or ties?

9. *Language of loss:* Do you understand how the language of loss has changed?

To clarify the last point, certain words are not used, such as "letting go," "moving on," "reinvesting in someone else," and even the much-used "closure." This is a word recently coined that implies there is a time limit and ending for grief. This is not in keeping with our ongoing enduring bond with loved ones. "Continual bonds" are far more in keeping with our belief in the communion of saints. Death is not the end of a relationship. Through prayerful remembrance we maintain a relationship with loved ones. Older psychological theories thought that ties had to be severed. Not to do so was considered abnormal or, worse, pathological. This is not held by new psychological "meaning centered" theories.

Attending to Your Loss History

We bring to our ministry the uniqueness of our own journey through grief. The more familiar we become with our own reactions and responses, the better we can console others. It is essential to keep in mind that our journey through grief colors the way we relate to others. If we have unresolved grief issues, our ministry will reflect it. It is also important not to become a grief minister who is working with the bereaved in order to resolve personal issues from the past. Resolving our loss problems will not happen that way, and it is not a healthy way to manage our own grief. In ministry there is always the important phrase that we have to keep in mind: "Whose needs am I serving?" In the process of discerning we must ask what is best for the other person, the community, and the church.

Loss Inventory for Grief Ministers

In reflecting on our own life's journey it is important that we identify our experiences that we bring to ministry. As you go through the inventory reflect on how your attitudes have or have not changed. Complete the following phrases:

1. I first learned about death and how it happens when . . .
2. At home we talked about death . . .
3. My belief in God affected my attitude toward death in the following ways . . .

4. When I first encountered death I felt . . .

5. Seeing others grieve makes me feel . . .

6. As an adult I want to console others because . . .

7. I think some of the difficulties in this ministry will be . . .

8. I believe I can console others in this ministry because . . .

9. Today for me death means . . .

Planning Grief Ministry

It is very helpful to carefully plan how grief ministry will occur. Ministerial moments clearly illustrate the many ministries that comprise the total ministry of consolation. Members of the believing community are called to certain aspects of this multifaceted ministry. The following will help those who want to minister in their discernment of what their role should be.

1. At the Time of Death (First-Response Ministry)

Who represents the parish at the deceased relative's home? Is there anyone who is prepared to help with basic activities such as phone calls and transportation to airports and railway stations? What about bringing by prepared food? Are you able to be quiet and be there helping with the nuts and bolts of notifications and first issues?

The ritual accompanying this time is called "Gathering Together in the Presence of the Body." Is there a pastoral minister or other member of the parish staff ready to be there at this time? During discernment it is helpful to revisit the ritual itself for gathering together with the family. Here a minister takes a role in nudging toward the spiritual.

2. Arranging the Funeral

Does the parish provide a booklet for effective planning? Does this booklet explain the liturgy and those who will participate and minister at the time of the funeral journey? Is there a parish staff person or member of the bereavement team who can assist families with options and ideas for the celebration of the funeral? Has this person been trained according to the church's funeral ritual *Order of Christian Funerals*? Do you feel comfortable with contacting the family and offering to assist with this?

3. The Vigil (formerly called the wake)

This is the first liturgical moment in the death of a Christian. According to the ritual this may be celebrated at the funeral home, the deceased's home, or the parish church. It should be explained to those who are mourning how the church celebration differs from the others. This liturgy needs to be carefully planned. Here ministries at the request of the family may take on a variety of roles from helping plan remembrances to offering prayers while the vigil takes place.

4. The Funeral and Afterwards (Liturgical Ministry)

The minister as ritual planner has already met with family members for planning the funeral Mass. There are specific options available in the ritual for lectors and family participation. Explaining the purpose and consolation of the signs and symbols surrounding the liturgy is very healing.[3] The consoling grief minister may act as facilitator in arranging for different roles. He or she may identify for the family how to consider filling such positions as pallbearers, lectors, offertory presenters. It is helpful to have a guide to work with in planning; my book *Planning the Catholic Funeral*[4] outlines significant ministries and participation for families. It is very helpful in accurately doing liturgical planning.

Ministers who want to help with the gathering after the funeral play an important role as healing ministers of hospitality. They may help prepare food for the occasion. The parish hall may be offered for this gathering.

5. Spiritual Guides (Guidance Ministry)

Parishes are willing to train individuals sensitive to the needs of the bereaved to be mentors. They act as spiritual guides to be there for the bereaved who need to have a one-to-one relation-

ship. This ties in with the minister as "compassionate listener."
Follow-up visits should occur two weeks to one month after the
death, along with an invitation to support groups.

6. Parish Support Group (Invitational Ministry)

The "support group" is often called by other names in parishes.
These are the more sophisticated groups led by a person with
professional credentials. In grief ministry the ideal is for parishes
to utilize professionals or trained facilitators from the parish to lead
a parish group. The group develops a covenant among its members to participate and help each other in the grieving process. A
variety of topics for discussion ranging from the descriptions of
grief to coping with holy days, holidays, and anniversaries may
be explored. There are many good books and articles on support
groups. This is not meant to be a therapy group.

7. Bereavement Committee (Administrative Ministry)

The parish bereavement committee works as a subcommit-
tee of the parish pastoral council. It helps to facilitate the entire
ministry of consolation in the parish. It is a vital committee for
initiating and supporting the bereaved in parish events ranging from anointing of the sick to special liturgies (November,
Advent, and Lent) and with special focus on groups often overlooked such as children and youth.[5] They help set the parish
calendar and coordinate ministries.

8. Professional Referrals (Healing Ministry)

It is important for a support group to be led by a professional
since it is dealing with intense issues. When there are mental
health issues that become paramount in response to grief, that
grief is characterized by the term "complicated." This means
that the bereaved need professional assistance in coping with
loss. There may well be an underlying depression or trauma,
which are difficulties in need of professional referral. Grief in
itself as a norm is not an illness. It is the response to what may
be a stress-filled loss. Other losses may be expected and are not

always as stressful. Parishes are more than capable in assisting people who are suffering from normal characteristics. There has to be a professional referral when it is evident that there is depression or other ways that demonstrate an inability to cope. Good referrals to professionals familiar with treatment for those suffering from complicated grief ought to be made. It is always best if the bereaved person with pastoral support makes the call her/himself for professional help. For the most part there are not large statistics associated with the need for referrals. It has been stated that only 15 percent need the referrals and that percentage is even disputed to be lower.

We cannot attend to the ministry of consolation without attending at the same time to ministers. Ministry and ministers define with God's help how consolation will take place for the bereaved.

Ministry Toolbox

1. All ministry requires ongoing support and formation.
2. There are choices as to how and where to minister in grief ministry.
3. Grief ministers have to be aware of their own experiences of loss.
4. Through praying for guidance and discerning with others we are better ministers. You may want your own loving listener for your ministry.
5. Always inquire as to what the institution (parish, college, hospital, etc.) will provide for ongoing formation in grief ministry.
6. Be aware that there is a major shift in models from "letting go" to "continual bonds."

2

Grief Minister as Helper

If one member [of the Body of Christ, which is the church,] suffers, all suffer together. (1 Cor 12:26)

We are called to console one another. Unfortunately, mistakes are made when inappropriate remarks or platitudes are offered. We, like our society, can be callous and expect people to "let go" of their grief quickly.

We need to cultivate ways to prepare ourselves to know how to respond. One of the best things we can do is to be reflective about our own experiences of loss and the way we either manage or fail to manage grief. While we do this, we ought to ask ourselves what comforts us and helps us put our grief into a broader spiritual perspective. When we are reflecting, we should not limit ourselves to the immediate experiences of intense grief. Rather, think about the times after the funeral is over, when life has returned to normal but then suddenly a sound, smell, or situation intensifies the lurking grief, bringing it to the fore once more. It is those times when we can insert our losses into a broader spiritual perspective by thinking of our loved one's place in the universe of God's love and our continual bond with them.

In situations where we want to help, we ought to keep in mind that the bereaved receive comfort from our being with them. Being with them is often enough. Better still is to help them express how they feel and talk out their loss.

Caring for the bereaved may entail everything from house-sitting to helping them make funeral arrangements. Instead of feeling paralyzed or empty when we encounter grief, we can experience God's love. Grief experiences are converted to hope when we allow ourselves to journey with the bereaved through darkness. We should try to give the bereaved permission to express feelings and know we are not going to tell them to "pull themselves together and don't cry." By letting the emotions out, we help them begin to experience new meaning and hope. The cleansing or "purification" relieves stress.

We know a lot more today about bereavement than in the past. Studies in crisis provide us with insights and ways to console ourselves and others. How we actually respond does make a considerable difference in the way anyone manages loss.

Grief Moments

Mourning the loss of a loved one is characterized by certain moments or times. It is difficult to assign rigid time limits to the phases as they differ due to our "loss histories." It is better to think of grief as certain times rather than rigid steps. When it comes to bereavement, we have to realize that there is no complete theory for grief. If there were a simple approach with a beginning, middle, and end, then all we really would need is just one book that would take care of everyone. We realize this is not the case nor will it ever be like that. One size does not fit all.

New literature emphasizes how our feelings oscillate between tears and laughter. God made us in such a way that our orienting to loss is lessened when we are able to laugh. I used to think that laughter was inappropriate, especially in church. Now, I realize it is often the way we cope between being shattered (tears) and being restored (rebuilding). It is very much the way we revise (what we assumed in our world would not change) and rebuild our lives (restoring). We go back and forth in our mood. This is a healing aspect of a good grief way of processing our thoughts and emotions. This is how we are able to regain our balance.

1. Early Moments (Time of Separation)

The earliest time may consist of numbness and shock and is best approached with an open mind. There may also be at this time the protesting of the loss, which may be exhibited through avoidance or denial. It is definitely a time that is disorienting. This disorientation is not illness. Rather, it is normal and to be expected in the face of the loss. *Always keep in mind that grief does not happen to us.* Rather, it is our perception of the loss that causes stress. It is not always the same for everyone. Some will experience stress reactions while others may not. It depends on the nature and ties we have with those who have died.

Allow the bereaved to grieve. Don't recommend alcohol or other drugs as a solution to grief feelings. If medical intervention is necessary, approach it cautiously with professional help. Alcohol and other drugs just mask very natural responses.

Don't be afraid to cry with the bereaved. Share your faith during this time in non-preachy ways. Offer to read the Bible with the bereaved or look over potential readings for the funeral if asked. Offer prayers with the bereaved. Simple prayers are best in these situations. Remember that familiar prayers comfort during confusing times. This is especially evident in hospice care. Grieving is not the severing of ties or bonds. At the heart of grief is the way we hope to rebuild meaning in our lives and maintain our enduring bond of love.

The intensity of grief gives way to a calmer period, allowing the bereaved to talk and reminisce about the past. When you share with them, you are helping them to redefine their relationship with the deceased. By doing so you are helping them alter their perspective. This is one of the most difficult challenges we associate with grief. It is essential that the bereaved accept and resolve loss by recalling memories and, through faith and experience, the hope that they will be reunited with their loved ones again in the kingdom. This recollection ought never to be forced. We give them the freedom to talk about what they want. In helping them in many ways we lead from behind. It is not necessary to remember everything or certain details. One psychologist, Robert Neimeyer, tells us that too much recollecting is like looking at the sun without eye protection. We hurt our eyes.

Awareness of Grieving Process

We do everything in our culture entirely too fast. We shop, eat, work, and even recreate at a very fast pace. Very often grief is treated in the same fashion. We do not allow people to really process their thoughts and feelings. Too much too soon is expected of them.

In the workplace we find that well-meaning coworkers may not know how to relate to the grief stricken. Very often they practice avoidance and denial. Others feel that in a matter of a few weeks everything is back to "normal," and many believe an even shorter time is all that is necessary for the bereaved to be over the grief. This illustrates that there is an ignorance in our society about the grieving process.

We must keep in mind that grief is an intensely personal response. There are still some overall characteristics that can help us to generally appreciate what is occuring with the bereaved. Grief may be cumulative, and how we have done in the past greatly affects grief's outcome. If there are many losses and we have had trouble accepting them, then it will certainly be more difficult.

Circumstances vary among losses. If there is a sudden death or death by violence (i.e., suicide or murder), the initial time of shock will be longer and more intense. We can expect someone to be numbed for a considerable time when the loss is someone with whom there is a strong affectional bond.

Descriptions Accompanying Loss

It cannot be emphasized enough that these are normal initial descriptions associated with grief. Only when they linger for a length of time beyond the initial time is there the possibility of more serious concerns. Then professional help may be needed.

As a mental health counselor I have counseled and facilitated numerous bereavement groups throughout the years. What I have always noticed is that the bereaved need reassurance that they are not mentally ill due to the way society describes it. Everyone can help by being aware of what is occurring for them while they grieve. Some possible early physical characteristics include the following:

- A tightness in the throat and heaviness in the chest
- Sighing
- An empty feeling in the stomach
- Loss of appetite or a desire to eat more
- Feelings of restlessness and looking for activity
- A desire to smoke, drink, or use drugs (especially tranquilizers)
- Difficulty in concentrating or staying focused
- Aimlessly wandering and forgetting to finish household chores
- Difficulty sleeping
- Need to tell and retell the story of the loved one's death
- Oscillating of moods (between being shattered and restored)
- Angry or agitated at the slightest things, even toward God
- Anger that is misdirected toward the wrong person
- Intensely angry at loved one for "having left"
- Crying at unexpected times
- Sensing the loved one's presence, hearing his or her voice
- Expecting the loved one to come home any minute
- Assuming mannerisms or traits of the loved one
- Yearning to be with the loved one or see him or her again

These are normal grief reactions as we initially experience the shock of realizing that our loved one has died. This is not an exhaustive list. It is meant to assist us with some overall aspects of initial loss. The grief minister in being aware of these reactions can expect them and consider how their impact determines the openness to ministry.

2. Another Moment (Transition)

After some time (may be months, weeks, or days) there may be a new realization that the loved one has died. Very often this is the time when the bereaved need the most help. They find themselves alone and aware that the death has occurred. We can help by keeping this in mind when we communicate with them. It is during this time when those who are mourning may well need a "compassionate listener." This listener will help them to sort out all of their feelings and accept the loss.

During this time, the numbness that seems to anesthetize the body wears off. Now certain emotions may surface such as anger, powerlessness, anxiety, guilt, or helplessness. On the other hand, resilience, adjustment, and acceptance may be what you encounter as a grief minister. Here again we are talking generally and this general perspective should always be kept in mind.

It is necessary for the bereaved to recall the loved one in many ways. There are very real changes in their minds about the loved one. They are moving in their thoughts from having someone who was physically present and now a new relationship continues. They need someone who is willing to be with them as the new story unfolds. (Chap. 10, "Grief Minister as Compassionate Listener," details this aspect of ministry.)

3. Moving Forward (Reorganizing One's Life)

This is when they start to readjust to their loss. Does this mean that grief has ended? The answer is no. There is no time limit for grief. After certain lengths of time it seems the bereaved usually are better able to cope. They are at a time when they can revisit activities they did in the past. Once again their lives are becoming manageable.

What to Expect (Important Scenarios Relating to the Grief Stricken)

While people continue living with loss there may be significant spiritual changes. There are many variables affecting people in differing ways. Some of the following apply in another inexhaustible list:

Separation

- Minister is there to reassure the bereaved
- Minister listens to losses (in empathic manner)
- Minister brings faith dimension (prayer and example)

Transition

- Minister is there to listen, offer perspective
- Minister offers prayer/spiritual guidance
- Minister helps place loss into context of faith

Reorganizing

- Anniversaries (awareness of "anniversary effect")
- Prayer (personal and liturgical)
- Coping (journal writing)
- Remembering with our ongoing "continual bond"

It is best to visualize the "grieving process" according to the above. There are many ways to talk about how we grieve. There are many ways to companion the bereaved. Some theories are more involved than others. This approach takes into account the chaos and even serenity. The following are scenarios of the first six weeks of grief and what people may go through early on while they grieve. You can develop this or some other kind of "grieving guide" to assist in the ministry. Again be aware that this may not apply to everyone.

Week One. Shock and numbness occur, followed by protest and denial. There are both physical and behavioral changes for the bereaved. We noted the physical. Some of the behavioral changes are the lack of focus evident in the inability to make decisions and feelings of being broken or shattered. Irritability is often exhibited due to the extreme stress. Look also for signs of being distracted. It is important that with the distractibility caution be taken, especially while driving a car or operating machinery. The minister needs to make allowances for this behavior, which can make attempts to minister difficult. Upsetting mannerisms such as sighing or crying can also impact a minister's willingness to "be there" for the people. On the other side of grief, none of this may apply to others who are bereaved. Their perception of the loss and worldview may manifest itself in differing ways. They may well be experiencing peace as they are comforted by living with the belief in a continual relationship. This is not something that needs to be "policed" by society. Policing entails heaped-up expectations upon the bereaved that do not necessarily apply. For the bereaved there are different ways of coping. We can never put people into structures that explain away everything. You can pretty well tell if they have a loss orientation or a restoring orientation. They may well change between the two orientations.

Week Two. Even though the funeral has taken place, there may still be strong feelings of "unreality." It is still difficult to accept that the death really has happened. The "wake" and funeral may take on a dreamlike quality that someone else experienced. There are financial and legal matters to take care of. By now the deceased's will has been read. In families there may be tension due to the last will and testament. Everything from anger to gratitude may be expressed.

Week Three. We must keep in mind when visiting the bereaved that grief is much more of a process we go through than the recollection of an event. It is still very early and the possible shock and numbness along with behavior has not noticeably changed. The bereaved are still trying to "sort things out." There is the hope to make some sense out of everything.

Week Four. We may encounter a yearning and searching by the bereaved for their loved one. At this point photographs or family albums may be opened. The spiritual wondering and need for prayer may surface in better ways now. There may well be the need to have some prayers to help match the bereaved's moods. Some ritualizing will take place with the "month's mind Mass."

Week Five. Feelings of isolation may be voiced from the bereaved. Staying at home alone may be a real burden. There may occur some mild confusion. The bereaved may still inadvertently think the loved one will call on the phone or come in the door any minute. They even pick up the phone to share something only to catch themselves and realize that the loved one has died. This can be very troubling for those attempting to relate to them and move the bereaved along in the process. It is very normal for this to happen. We need not be overly concerned.

Week Six. It may take this long or even longer before the bereaved are ready to seek some help. Help may appear with someone willing to visit and be a "compassionate listener" or by joining a "prayer or support group." Now the bereaved may start to become proactive and seek some direction living with grief.

Grief touches all of us in a variety of ways. Grief similar to our own is unique. As we noted, "one size does not fit all." However, there are aspects that we share in common. Dealing with our emotions as grief ministers is a formidable challenge as we reach out to help those who are mourning. It is a special time of self-discovery and transformation for the bereaved and also for ourselves while we minister.

Developing Skills for Ministry

One of the most difficult encounters we may face is how to relate well to the bereaved. People agonize over the right words for the condolence cards or a conversation they may have with the bereaved. This ministry is avoided by many not out of a lack of concern as much as an anxiousness and fear of doing or saying the wrong thing.

The anxiousness experienced by people about bereavement highlights the need for developing skills in communicating. Considerable anxiety may be avoided when we catechize or teach others how to go through life events and find meaning. As a church we have to be careful not to contribute to secular frameworks for grief. Preparation for ministry training and acquiring healing skills has to be provided. Role playing and appreciating what it means to be with the bereaved can make people more effective and caring ministers.

The following scenario illustrates the need for proper ministry formation and reflection.

Conversing with the Bereaved

Grief Minister (G.M.): "Hello, Brenda, I just thought I'd give you a call to keep in contact."

Brenda: "Everything's going along."

G.M.: "Are you getting things done?"

Brenda: "I'm not sure about a lot of things. It's pretty confusing."

G.M.: "It's still very early for you."

Brenda: "I am trying to adjust."

G.M.: "I'd like to drop by to see you."

Brenda: "That's really kind of you. I think I really need company."

This conversation is a brief way of offering some possible conversations with the bereaved. It requires that the grief minister who wants to be of help be aware of how a conversation could likely take place. It also sharpens ministry listening skills. What did you really hear now that you are better acquainted with thoughts and feelings? How well did you listen to the bereaved's needs? Did you use open-ended statements in order to better engage the bereaved person? These are just a few of the questions and observations for a pastoral ministry formation seminar. The questions are open-ended and will inspire more remarks and observations for the ministry.

In chapter 10, which is entitled "Grief Minister as Compassionate Listener," we will explore in detail the importance of developing better listening skills for ministry. Listening and being present to others while they grieve has been called the silent side of communication. It is this ministry of being a healing presence to the bereaved that is most helpful. No one should shy away from this as it is a very rewarding skill that needs to be acquired.

Is There a Time Limit for Grief?

Many questions surface as we begin grief ministry. The bereaved often ask the question about when this will all be over. It is very important that the bereaved not be misled. There really is no time limit, as is evidenced by anniversaries. Anniversaries are a major concern for grief ministers ("anniversary effect" is treated in chap. 7).

Anniversaries are the best way of showing how grief has no time limit. All of us are aware of certain dates and times of the year when we recall our loved ones who have died. The more sensitive we are to this reality, the better we can be caring and empathic toward the grief stricken. Going through the process we learn that bereavement is something we accept; we will never fully "get over it." Rather we learn to cope in better ways with loss. This is especially true of those whose loved one's death has caused a change in their life condition. When someone becomes a widow or widower, he or she doesn't cease to be one after so much time has elapsed, and has learned to cope with the new status. This new status was especially important in the early church when there was the order of widows—those who had gone through bereavement and were now able to help others because of their empathy and living in the Christian community.

Needed Resources for Grief Ministry

Losing a loved one may be a shattering experience. We need to call upon resources that help the bereaved to rebuild trust and hope. Immediately following the terrible events of catastrophies and terrorism, there were many prayer services and words of consolation. A considerable amount of hope continues to be given to the families of victims in those early words and prayers that stay with them in their extended time of bereavement. The prayers and psalms offer the bereaved a context to accompany them in grieving. As such these initial comforting words become a touchstone to return to in the times of stress and loss, whether it is a week, a decade, or a lifetime since the loss.

In grief ministry the psalms are a cornerstone for both the bereaved and the compassionate minister's encounters with grief. The psalms play a large role in the formation of the grief minister who acts as a "spiritual guide." (Chap. 6 treats spiritual expression and chap. 3 spiritual guides.)

We have noted the importance of children and teenagers in grief ministry. During the anniversaries of tragic events, children are often included in the remembrance ceremonies. It is heartrending to see them read names of victims, including their own fathers, mothers, siblings, grandparents, aunts, uncles, and friends. We cannot help but feel the pain of families who suffer such a tragedy.

This emphasis on children focuses our sympathies on the young who have suffered, but at the same time we are hopeful that these children will cope and grow in their spiritual development just as they develop physically. Seeing the young, we are always hopeful of the promise of emerging life (chap. 4 will detail the role of the grief minister and the grieving child).

The ministry of consolation is a multifaceted experience of service in the church. As a ministry it serves a variety of intense needs facing community members while they struggle with life's separation and loss.

Effective ministry requires that we connect our very selves to what we say and do. Our being present to others is an intensely spiritual reality that must be grounded in appreciating our life story as we listen to others. Here are some dos and don'ts that relate to how we are present to others.

Dos and Don'ts (The Importance of Being in the Right Framework for Ministry)

Some dos and don'ts can serve as a framework for familiarizing ourselves with better ways to bring healing and hope for the bereaved.

Be present as soon as possible when you hear about a death.

Avoid offering platitudes. Such remarks as "It's all for the best," "It was meant to happen," or even "It's God's will" are untimely for the bereaved. While ultimately they do have to accept and, with God's help, they will accept that death has occurred, they still need to process that acceptance.

Do not simply offer "sympathy." Be empathic. This means placing yourself in the other person's position. Rather than saying, "I am sorry," it is better to say, "This must be very difficult." The latter is more engaging. Use open-ended questions such as, "How are you doing today?"

After the funeral realize that the bereaved still need to tell the story of loss. They need to ritualize the loss. This may entail looking at photographs or praying with them at the cemetery.

Become more familiar with the "grieving process." Appreciate that it is part of the life cycle. There is a spirituality to be cultivated with life's losses.

Rituals redefine new relationships with the deceased.

Anniversaries, family celebrations, and holidays need to include ways of remembering the deceased in the context of the Body of Christ.

Don't buy into society's time frames. You know from your own experience how long grief lasts. Don't avoid the subject because the loss was a month or two ago or even ten or more years ago.

Inquire how everything is going. If you feel close to the person offer to help with chores that have to be accomplished. You may offer to help clean or deliver clothes and other possessions to the St. Vincent de Paul Society, Catholic Charities, or other suitable charities.

These are a few ways that we can begin to reassess how we bring care and comfort to those who are suffering losses. In doing so we also bring images of healing and hope into own lives. Relating in purposeful ways brings light to the otherwise possible darkness and chaos of intense loss.

Ministry Toolbox

In your ministry be aware that there does exist the other side of grief. The following points are important to keep in mind:

People have feelings of relief that their loved one's suffering has ended.

Some bereaved find themselves more resilient than they thought.

Many are comforted by assurances of faith.

Belief in the hope of seeing loved ones again in the kingdom is comforting and consoling.

Be aware that the dominant theories are about relinquishing and letting go, whereas the new psychology encourages new ways to maintain relationships with those who go before us in faith through prayer (as spiritual conversing).

Not everyone cries.

Recognize that there is deep belief in an "enduring" or "continual bond." This has always been evident, yet the relinquishing theories did not notice this.

3

Grief Minister as Spiritual Guide

The LORD is my shepherd, I shall not want.
    He makes me lie down in green pastures;
he leads me beside still waters;
    he restores my soul. (Ps 23:1-3)

Being a grief minister requires ongoing formation. A major concern is the ongoing development of a spiritual outlook toward life. This ministry is very involved with spiritual matters facing both grief ministers and those whom they serve.

Throughout the years I've been ministering to the bereaved, I have heard whispers about grief ministry being depressing or negative. Some have even ventured to ask me, "How can you do the work you do? It must be very depressing to deal with death?" How far from the truth are such remarks! My response has always been that this ministry is about life, not death. It is eternal life and the consolation of believing in the reign of God.

Questions about this ministry and its meaning continue in our society, which is in so much need of evangelization. Proclaiming and living the spirituality of this ministry gives the world a witness to eternal spiritual values. Spiritual guidance and prayer are cornerstones for every ministry. This chapter highlights how spiritual guidance is an essential part of grief ministry. All that we do and say throughout bereavement ministry focuses on how well we provide consolation from the Source of all consolation.

Grief ministry is synonymous with the ministry of consolation. It is in the consoling that we find the spiritual guidance from the One who gives us all consolation and hope. Providing spiritual guidance is not so much a learned skill as it is a gift. It involves being with people and involves listening and hearing. It is more often the singer and not the song. It is sharing faith, not knowledge. The grief minister brings his or her compassionate vision of life to those whose lives are out of focus or who can try to see only through their tears. The grief minister is a guide and companion for those who are trying to sort out what living with loss now means for them.

Offering Guidance

Gerald May, in his *Care of Mind, Care of Spirit: A Psychiatrist Explores Spiritual Direction*, gives us the following words about who provides spiritual guidance:

> Spiritual guidance can apply to any situation in which people receive help, assistance, attention, or facilitation in the process of their spiritual formation. This applies not only to deepening one's personal realization of a relationship to God, but also to the dynamic living-out of that realization in the actions of daily life. Spiritual guidance can come through almost any conceivable channel. Certainly it can occur in the church or other religious community settings, but it can also come from friends, family, co-workers, scripture, nature, art, and a multitude of other sources.[1]

Spiritual Needs during Hospice Care

Spiritual guidance is necessary when loss occurs. This may be when a family first hears a diagnosis. Guidance is needed for the patient and the family to go through the experience. This guidance may take the form of helping everyone to accept and care for each other as Christians. Individuals and families are thrown off balance when end-of-life illnesses and issues occur.

During hospice care we find many examples of the need for spiritual guidance. Hospice care specializes in care for patients and families. This is when life-limiting illness no longer responds to treatments seeking to cure the sick person. Hospice acknowledges that life is finite and that at a certain point medical interventions will not restore physical health. Acknowledging this end means that the focus is now on comfort and preparation for both the patient and his or her family. The hospice worker may well be a grief minister who acts in many ways as a spiritual and emotional guide for the person's final journey.

During the time of serious illness and the death of a loved one, many cries for spiritual guidance may happen. The grief minister often functions as helper, compassionate listener, ritual planner, and often a friend during bereavement. A spiritual guide—by his or her presence, listening, and words—offers guidance. On occasion there will be questions about God, the afterlife, suffering, forgiveness, guilt, and other spiritual topics. Questions or remarks may surface when we least expect it. The hope is in preparing for the ministry with other ministers that the grief minister will discuss spiritual situations facing the bereaved and strategize on helpful interventions. These are the significant conversations that have to happen.

Companioning

The spiritual guide is not there to give answers or rescue the bereaved from their fears and doubts. Effective guides are those who assist the grief stricken in activating their inner resources of faith and trust in order to welcome into their lives more spiritual ways of coping. Guides are there to help the bereaved as companions who show them the way, sometimes not even with words. They are a spiritual presence, reminding the bereaved that they have the spiritual support of the entire community. The grief minister, as a representative of the community, is sharing with the bereaved the church's compassionate vision of hope. Carolyn Gratton, in *The Art of Spiritual Guidance*, clearly spells out what being a spiritual guide entails: "The guide is there to help with the interpretation of present crises or transitions, both by stimulating the person's own imagination and empowering him or her to appraise a new vision for the future."[2]

The guide is most helpful when he or she has lived through a time of searching for meaning. When the guide is one who has had to overcome emptiness, anger, searching, guilt, feelings of abandonment, and so many other aspects of loss by going through this, he or she becomes a better instrument for contributing to the spiritual well-being of the bereaved.

Pastoral Moments and Guidance

Ministry to the bereaved, as with many pastoral moments, requires guidance. Spiritual guidance is sought by those who want to know what they need to do for their loved ones and themselves. Let us look at a few of these times, keeping in mind that the grief minister is there to recognize crises and give spiritual guidance and direction.

Early Moments

These moments occur when we first hear about someone who is seriously ill in the parish. The grief minister as pastoral visitor assists families with spiritual and sacramental matters. When the grief minister is familiar with the sacrament of the sick, he or she can be very helpful. In keeping with the words of the apostle James, "Are any among you sick? They should call for the elders of the church" (Jas 5:14), the grief minister can be the one who helps families call for the anointing. This is especially timely in hospice care.

When there is serious illness, families often begin to become paralyzed as to what to do. They are in need of guidance as they anticipate the death of a loved one. Halting, confused conversations about the funeral take place. There is often guilt at thinking about addressing future arrangements. At that time the loved one's journey in life is vivid for the bereaved. They are in need of a personal caring way to live through these difficult moments.

The grief minister is one who listens and offers ways to express love for the loved one at the end of life and in death. When the grief minister has already visited the family before the death occurs, it is much easier to offer spiritual guidance. There is a connection with the family who see this person as someone who was with them in their difficult times.

Throughout the two days of the funeral the church fills the time with prayers for the deceased Christian. It is the grief minister who gives guidance to families who may not have had a funeral in years. Grief at this time can be very chaotic and confusing. When the grief minister is available during the rites, his or her presence offers spiritual guidance.[3]

Condolence Call

Within the first few weeks after a death a condolence call to the bereaved may be scheduled. At that time the grief minister visits with the grieving parishioner and is supportive. It is still very early for the bereaved in their grieving experience. Certain questions may surface at this time. Some of the questions are painful, such as, "Why did he have to leave me?" "Did I do something wrong for this to happen?" "Will I ever see her again?"

The grief minister is not there to give answers or rescue the bereaved from fears and doubts. Rather, he or she is there to help them move through their grief. It may well be a time when the grief minister will pray with the bereaved not only for the deceased person but also for those left behind. This certainly assists the bereaved in the transition of accepting what has happened and placing it into the wider context of religious faith, hope, and love.

Anniversaries and Holidays

Guidance is given by the grief minister as time goes by for the bereaved. There are occasions when a pastoral visit is welcomed by the bereaved. Certain anniversaries such as birthdays, wedding anniversaries, and general holidays are always noted as difficult for the bereaved. They need to live through these times with both spiritual and social guidance. The visit at the time of the yearly anniversary Mass is a pastoral moment that brings healing and hope. Those who are suffering their loss now very quietly realize that their faith community has not forgotten their loved one (see chap. 7).

Gift of Ministry to the Bereaved

By virtue of our baptism we are given the spiritual gift to be instruments of healing to others. We are empowered to be with others in their times of suffering and joy. It cannot be emphasized enough that this is a gift. It is a gift to be given away for our own good and the good of the church. The grief minister need not be overly concerned about training and learning skills. He or she can be helpful, but what is most necessary is a willingness to assist the bereaved in developing a more spiritual relationship with God.

Spiritual Transformations

Many changes in outlook occur during bereavement. Grief ministry brings us to a point in our lives where we become more reflective. Ministering to others widens our horizons. As ministers it is important for us to consider the spiritual matters that may come up for the bereaved. We are then better able to reflect and prepare for our guiding ministry. Some of the following spiritual matters are prevalent for those who are grieving. Each of these is placed in a category in the grieving process. It is good to note whether this matter is brought up *early, mid, or later* in bereavement.

Wanting to Cry Out to God

(This we often find in early and mid grief.) For some there are strong feelings of being abandoned by God. They need permission to cry out from the depth of their being. They need someone to hear them express their innermost feelings of pain and suffering due to a loved one's death.

Feelings of Anger toward God

(This is early to mid grief.) It is not easy for a person of faith to hear someone express anger toward God. We must keep in mind that these are raw emotions trying to find meaning. The grief minister has to remember that the person needs to do this. Always keep in mind that they cannot harm God. Rather, expressing hurt is in reality the beginning of a *dialogue* with God.

Deep Sense of the Ultimacy of Life

(This is more reflective and probably occurs in mid and later grief.) The bereaved are aware that life is eternal as they mourn the death of a loved one. This is fueled by a belief system that gives them hope in meeting their loved one again in the reign of God. This spiritual belief has been called the "heavenly reunion." We hear this spiritual acceptance being voiced in support or grief seminars or parish support groups about a month to two months after the loss.

Better Detachment from Material Things

(This is evident very often during mid to later grief.) The beginning of spirituality is to recognize our dependence upon God. Good spiritual grief means that there is acceptance of our own powerlessness. Our lives are turned over to God. Spiritual guidance will emphasize our need for *surrendering*. Let's consider what Henri Nouwen has written about our "powerlessness" and learning to trust: "Start simply by admitting that you cannot cure yourself. You have to say yes fully to your powerlessness in order to let God heal you. But it is not really a question of first and then. Your willingness to experience your powerlessness already includes the beginning of surrendering to God's action in you."[4]

This guidance is in accord with surrendering as the beginning of experiencing spiritual growth. Twelve-step programs for addictions often acknowledge the "spiritual component" of our lives. As such the spiritual is the keystone—acknowledging that we cannot do anything apart from God. Twelve-step programs are spiritual and begin with this as the first step. This step approach has been adapted for ways to spiritually manage our losses.[5]

Search for Connectedness

(This is noted in mid to late grief.) Searching and yearning is one of the most prevalent spiritual feelings associated with loss. A bond may seem to be broken. Like a shattered vase, the bereaved person wants to find some meaning amid the emptiness. We've been told about "letting go." Now we find more hope in maintaining *continual bonds.* It is that we do not "let go" into a void. Rather, we maintain a new relationship in faith with our loved ones. In emptying ourselves we find fulfillment. In dying we rise. All of this amplifies the centrality of spirituality and connectedness while we grieve. At the heart of grief is not disengaging but rather it is finding meaning.

Developing a Spiritual Inventory

A spiritual inventory is helpful for the grief minister as he or she ponders the possibilities of the spiritual unrest in others. It makes us more aware of how we deal with grief in our own journey. Oftentimes the spiritual guidance we offer needs to be done according to the gifts given to us in our life's journey. We are pursuing what it means to meet the spiritual needs of the bereaved and offer our strength for them. Looking at how we are doing with some of our concerns and where we are receiving guidance is very helpful. Spiritual inventories shared with other grief ministers during planning sessions can be an invaluable tool for God's grace as we share our journey and best practices with others.

Ministry Toolbox

A Spiritual Inventory

While we minister it is a good idea to develop our own inventory. When we write this down, the answers are visible for us.

1. How do I think about God's will?

2. Do I connect Jesus' suffering with my own?

3. Do I blame God or others for death?

4. Do I consciously or unconsciously blame my loved one for leaving me?

5. Do I feel angry, guilty, or abandoned by everyone?

6. Do I need forgiveness from my deceased loved one?

7. Do I need to forgive my deceased loved one?

8. Have I tried to channel my spiritual feelings of emptiness into prayer or meditation? How do I maintain a "spiritual bond" with loved ones?

9. List three things I do that I find spiritually comforting.

10. List what I believe are spiritual resources for resilience to cope with loss.

4

Grief Minister and
the Grieving Child

*Let the little children come to me, and do not stop them;
for it is to such as these that the kingdom of heaven belongs.*
(Matt 19:14)

Ministry to grieving children requires preparation and formation. Grief ministers are more challenged in this ministry than many other areas of concern with life's separations and losses. Far too often children are overlooked during bereavement. Our goal has to be to include them and gain insights on how we can become more effective in ministering to children who grieve.

Helping children cope with the loss of a loved one through death is clearly a critical situation. The parish is a setting for healing this grief. Comfort and consolation through religious faith brings the healing reality of God's love to the child.

Children respond in a variety of ways to the death of a loved one. The Child Bereavement Study (1996), conducted at Massachusetts General Hospital in Boston by well-respected and leading researchers, found that both bereaved adults and bereaved children were struggling to find a way of maintaining a connection to the deceased. The researchers from the hospital and Harvard Medical School with new data were compelled to make necessary changes as to how we relate to grieving children and adults. This research shook the foundation of existing theories of stages, phases, and tasks, and created new structures for understanding grief. The researchers made known new findings:

> As each of us looked at data from our respective research we realized that we were observing phenomena that could not be accounted for within models of grief that most of our colleagues were using. It appeared that what we were observing was not a stage of disengagement, which we were educated to expect, but rather, we were observing people altering and then continuing their relationship to the lost person. Remaining connected seemed to facilitate both adults' and children's ability to cope with the loss and the accompanying changes in their lives. These 'connections' provided solace, comfort, and support, and eased the transition from the past to the future.[1]

Children observe events but cannot always interpret them. The more familiar grief ministers are with the way children grieve, the better they can help. Very often the child's response to death is startling. We may not expect to see the child "play funeral" or write a letter to Grandpa. The way children think about and imagine death is very important for adult grief ministers and parents to grasp.

Even though a five-year-old thinks of death as irreversible, very often she or he thinks that you can outwit it. "If Mommy was faster, she would not have died." The typical five- or six-year-old has confidence in her or his abilities. Death can be overcome. As children mature we encounter change in their perception of death. The eight-year-old's response might be, "Will we still have a vacation now that Nana has died?" There is a developmental need for children to realize how life will change for them. They are appropriately egocentric in the face of separation and loss.

The child gives way to the adolescent. Peer group pressure influences remarks. "Only my father died; none of my friends have had this happen." He or she is reluctant to show emotions. After all, the adolescent may have only recently learned to control emotions.

Through the Eyes of a Child

Often adults do not include children in the grieving process. Children have to be involved in the process of expressing their loss just the same as everyone else. We have to keep in mind that unresolved grief responses from childhood may affect them in later years. We must try to perceive grief through the eyes of a child.[2]

In age-appropriate ways it is necessary for grief ministers to familiarize themselves with how children respond to grief. An important dialogue between pastoral care and developmental psychology ought to be taking place. The parish is the appropriate place for speakers and seminars on loss and the coping mechanisms children utilize in the face of loss. Such training will go far with those who seek to assist children experiencing loss. One of the best approaches is with expressive therapy through art. It communicates what the child may be unable to verbalize.

Children go through what is known as "magical thinking."[3] When children misinterpret or distort reality, magical thinking takes over. Children may think that because they refused to kiss Nana good-bye, they are responsible for her death. Children will give us clues about their perception. For our part we need to pay attention. When we realize this, our intervention is critical. We need to describe death in concrete ways to children. We live in a death-denying culture. Parents and adults have to honestly answer children's questions. We need to learn to be direct and precise in our responses. We can't use euphemisms. They are inappropriate, and children will only become confused as they often take what is said literally. The cultural framework of "letting go" does not help children or adults.

Be Forthright

If we are avoiding painful questions asked in innocence, we have to ask ourselves that basic ministry question: "Whose needs am I serving?" We can easily placate ourselves and our own denial. Our avoidance of what is difficult to communicate to children only creates problems later on. This means telling them the actual physical causes of the death. "Nana's heart was just too weak to keep beating."

While it may be comforting for us to say, "God loved Nana so much that he took her to heaven," it does not work for children. Children think in concrete terms and tend to see God picking people out to take with him. "Maybe this God will take me next since Nana loved me."

Children search for the causes of a death. Language is very important in communicating with a child. To tell a child that his or her father has "gone away" or that he is "asleep" creates crises: "Why can't I wake him up?" "Did I do something wrong to have him go away?" "Was I so bad that he never wants to see me again?"

Redefining Relationships

The earlier a child ritualizes a loss, the better he or she does in the grieving process. "Letting go" really has to be replaced with new ways of connecting. Our responsibility as a church is to show how maintaining a bond is now possible. In order to do this we must be cautious that we do not become part of the problem.

A continual relationship may mean especially for the child a new way of imagining God, heaven, and the deceased loved one. Everything is different and the way we relate this is important for emotional and spiritual growth. Imagine the harm that is done when someone makes inappropriate remarks: "You are now the man of the family." "Boys don't cry." Or perhaps the most theologically difficult one of all: "God took him."

God's image is not enhanced when we avoid secondary causes. It is better to explain to the child once again that something went wrong: "The car was in an accident." "The heart stopped beating." "There was too much sickness, and her body could no longer handle it."

The image of God who loves and cares for us must always be reinforced. We do not want to attribute the origin of suffering and pain to God. After all, the Christian message is the alleviation of suffering. It will be very difficult for the child to relate to God when we even inadvertently make God the cause of pain and suffering. The child will wonder about this type of God: "Is God going to take me next?" The concrete explanation of causes is still the best one for children.

In talking with a child it is important that there be a setting where we can safely communicate about death. Children ought to be encouraged to express how they feel about the death of a grandparent, parent, uncle, or aunt. We also ought not to overlook the death of classmates or certainly a sibling. There is nothing worse than acting as if all losses are the same.

Children and Rituals

Opportunities for ritualizing losses create considerable healing. Rituals are healing vehicles for expressing ourselves and maintaining relationships. Children, like adults, need to ritualize. Research (as previously noted) shows that maintaining an ongoing bond with the deceased loved one is very beneficial for children. Our theology certainly provides many ways to appreciate heaven and the communion of saints. We have times in our liturgical calendar (especially November) when parish prayer services can be offered.[4] Children can also ritualize any past losses through simple prayer services. These can range from a remembrance ritual of recalling people who are gone to recalling favorite pets, and even lost objects that could be special toys.

We do not have to wait for a death to examine loss and how Christians come to view it. Grief ministers deal with loss not only when it occurs but also at liturgically correct times of the year. A simple lesson about the loss of a pet can go far in helping a child cope with major losses in life. Mister Rogers, the deceased television host and Presbyterian minister, did this with his stories about the death of a goldfish.

In the *Order of Christian Funerals* ministry and participation is emphasized throughout the ritual.[5] The community is encouraged to appreciate the sacred symbols and to express loss from the very beginning during specific moments in the funeral journey. The metaphor of journey is very practical and helpful for parishes. We are all journeying together as a pilgrim people no matter what our age. This concept, easily grasped by both children and adults, is a rich vehicle for teaching about life and death.

Children and Funerals

Among professionals there is overwhelming agreement that children three years and older can go to funerals. This means the vigil and the cemetery as well. It is, as one professional puts it, the teachable moment. "One should encourage children to express even fear, doubt, and curiosity, as well as being open to express one's own feelings concerning death."[6] Another keen insight about children and the funeral is made by Rabbi Earl Grollman. He makes a point that certainly speaks to a child's curiosity and imagination when he tells us that the burial is the best audiovisual aid in the world.[7] A child knows definitively where a person's body is. The question of viewing the body remains is best dealt with on a personal basis. If children express much interest in going, they should be allowed to do so for a short time. If children do not want to go, they should never be forced to do so.

Helping Children with Funerals

Parents have to look for help when it comes to guiding children with the funeral. If the death greatly affects the parents, there is all the more reason to seek out the grief minister. The grief minister is the one who can explain the funeral to children. At the same time by so doing he or she helps adults. After all, adults probably never received this help when they were children.

The grief minister, in helping children, often becomes a role model for the grieving children. The minister is the one who helped them through a very difficult time. In the days, weeks, and months ahead this will not be forgotten. For that matter the grief minister truly becomes one who shapes a lasting child-hood memory.

Explaining What Happens

Explaining does not mean the pouring out of information. It is really much more than that. The way the grief minister prepares and talks about the funeral communicates deep impressions on children. The following points will help:

1. What to expect? Unless the children have previously attended a funeral, they really are not aware of what happens. The minister needs to explain everything that occurs throughout the time of the funeral. Children will naturally come up with questions. Their questions become the way the minister comes to realize what the children are wondering about.

2. Fill the children in with specific descriptions. Tell them what to expect in the funeral home. Funeral directors can be very helpful in allowing children to visit early. They also are aware of how to talk with children. The grief minister has to remember to give children very concrete answers. Explain that the body is there and the soul has left the body. The deceased loved one is not asleep—rather his or her soul is with God.

3. You may have to field some unusual questions depending on how old the children are. They may want to know more about what death is like.

4. Explain that people cry because they miss the deceased loved one. It's all right to cry then and later.

5. Explain that the purpose of the funeral is to pray for the deceased relative to be happy with God. When children view the body, they may want to touch it to say good-bye. It is all right for them to do so. It is probably a good idea to reflect as they do so that when people die their bodies are cold and not to be alarmed by that.

I recall being at a family funeral and noticing that my twelve-year-old nephew stayed in the back of the room. His parents were very wise as they told him, "You can go up front when you are ready." They didn't overact in any way. Eventually I saw my nephew kneeling down by the casket and making the sign of the cross. He really took everything in and knew what to do by observing. This made him far more secure and aware of what he would do. He loved his grandmother and was able to express it.

Grief Ministry and Rituals

Rituals are pastoral care. The grief minister should avoid thinking of them as something separate that takes place before we start ministering.[8] In the *Order of Christian Funerals* we have a resource for expressing loss. The prayers and symbols are comforting for all ages. Explaining the symbols and readings to children is a way of bridging the gap between ritual and pastoral care.

Funerals are not only an adult experience. They affect all and as such they need to acknowledge everyone, including children. While it is not appropriate or practical to make a funeral into a children's liturgy, children, however, can and should have an active role in it. They should be encouraged to present the gifts, including personal drawings or statements about or for the deceased. By including children in the ritual, we not only address their feelings; we also send a powerful message to the rest of the mourners. While we journey some leave us and others join, but we are all traveling together toward the kingdom. The chain of our families from our distant ancestors before us to our descendants not yet born are together heading for the new and eternal Jerusalem.

A Ministry That Includes

Going through grief is appreciating our belief about life in the Spirit. As with all grief ministry, its purpose is to bring life and hope and to bring it more abundantly. Without some explanations and prayer services being offered to our young people, we set the stage for further denial and unresolved grief. Such a future ought not to happen. We Christians are suitably equipped to meet the needs of the bereaved in ways far better than our society. Not only does our pastoral theology help contribute meaning, so too does our pastoral psychology.

Through the signs and symbols ritualized in our funeral liturgies, we begin the mourning process in a spiritually enriching and comforting way. We allow young people to participate in ways that stimulate the expression of feelings. Such an expression is cathartic and healing. Our liturgies are meant to release, not control or block, our emotions.

Liturgies are not separate from our children. They serve them as well. When we teach our children, we must also care for them no matter what age or condition. In caring we include them in the rich tapestry of the church's education, life, and ritual, remembering that they too are our fellow pilgrims.

In conclusion, the following summations in this ministry toolbox explain how children and young people experience death in age-appropriate ways.

Ministry Toolbox

Infancy to Early Childhood

Even in infancy there is a sense of loss. Infants certainly do not understand death. However, they experience separation and loss. They learn early on about permanence and separation. This is demonstrated in what may well be their first ritual: "Peekaboo."

Preschool

At around age four there is the realization that something has happened. However, death is seen as only temporary. Children may expect the deceased person to wake up and play with them. Again the usage of correct language about loss with children is very important.

Elementary School

It is still important that we attribute the right causes of death for children. It is equally important that children be included in the funeral rituals. Their participation or exclusion plays an important role in their growth and future grief management. The grief minister must always keep in mind that working with the parents is the way decisions have to be made. Parents have to be encouraged to talk with their grieving children about going to the funeral.

Adolescence

Death as a social dimension is very real in teenagers' lives. The expression of emotions requires considerable patience by adults. We need to learn how to read what adolescents are really trying to tell us. This is a critical time when questions about the very purpose of living are being raised in adolescents' minds.

5

Grief Minister and Teenage Loss

The LORD is good to those who wait for him,
to the soul that seeks him.
It is good that one should wait quietly
for the salvation of the LORD. (Lam 3:25-26)

Experiences of separation and loss occur at any time in our lives. We realize that grief is an intensely personal experience. There are characteristics that we share in common. For grief ministers it is very important not to overlook where we are in age and maturity.[1] It does matter where we are in our lives. Descriptions of grief for an older person are noticeably different from those of a child. Similarly the experience of loss for a teenager, while sharing in common characteristics, is noticeably different. It is unfortunate that far too often the teenager is the person excluded or overlooked in our society.

Recent notice has been given to teenagers due to depression. The unhealthy acting out of teenage depression has alarmed us, with harm in the form of death from suicide taking place among this young segment of our society. Our society needs to be more aware of teenage grief and the very definite needs facing teens as they confront loss.

Ministers who console have to address the needs facing bereaved teenagers. The Gospel has to speak to the point of their needs. It is through the Word taking form in pastoral care seminars, counseling, and creating an atmosphere of concern that teenagers are able to place their loss into the context of faith.

It is no easy task for grief ministers to relate to bereaved teenagers. Their needs are very complex and they do not always verbalize what is bothering them. The following pastoral example illustrates how the loss of a sibling affected a teenager:

Mary Ellen came by to talk about her sadness over the loss of her brother four years ago. As we talked she noted that she had just celebrated her birthday. She was now a year older than her brother when he died. She had outlived him now even in terms of birthdays. This meant she had to work on developing an entirely new image and relationship with him in death.

Different Aspects of Teenage Grief

Grief ministers have to be aware that teenage grief shares common characteristics with other age groups. What makes it different are factors concerned with psychological and physical growth. Similar to everyone, teenagers are a product of what is happening to them physically and emotionally. The teenage years are in themselves a time of transition. It is not by accident that many cultures have *rites of passage* for this age group. Somehow what has to be demonstrated is that they are now moving into adulthood. It is a time of intense stress as teenagers wonder not only about physical developments but emotional ones of separating from the security of childhood. They have to assert that they are independent, even though they may have very real misgivings. To complicate matters they have peers who also assert pressure. Culturally there are many expectations heaped upon teenagers.

When I first was studying psychology, I recall a professor giving a very good definition of adolescence. He said that "adolescence is like taking a house with all the furniture in it and moving it across the street." Over the years I've seen this definition ring true for teenagers. It is really a chaotic time. We have to expect everything to be moved around during the transition.

Grief is a chaotic time and sorting everything out is no easy accomplishment. When grief strikes the teenager, we have to make certain accommodations. The more we are aware of what is occurring with the teenager, the better we are able to be supportive.

Charting Teenage Loss

Grief ministry has the awareness that the better prepared we are for loss, then the better we will cope. This in no way minimizes the intensity of the moment of loss despite how much we anticipate it. The anticipated loss suddenly becomes very real and final. Being prepared does, however, help since we've already anticipated the patterns of our response to loss.

Sudden death, however, is very much in a category all its own. We note this especially when a teenager dies in an automobile accident. It is so unexpected by teenagers who grieve the loss of a friend that the shock is very intense. Most aware communities respond with opening up schools and having crisis counselors talk with bereaved students. Teens, being very peer-related, do well in this setting where they can get help while being with other bereaved teens.

Teenagers feel the pressure of prolonged illness. Whether it is a sibling or a parent, such illness affects them deeply. At the same time there is not always the demonstration of emotion. We have to be aware that they are still trying to assume an image of adulthood. Consequently it seems to take longer to see them grieve. Without a societal norm for grief or clear expectations in a death-denying culture, teens seem to flounder more than the rest of us. In the face of such confusion, they opt for control of emotions, denial, and an apparent uncaring attitude amid very real suffering.

The grief minister wanting to chart grief can utilize the moments of grief as they apply to teenagers. This will greatly aid the grief minister in anticipating the losses as the teenager goes through a grieving process. If we look briefly at the initial time, transitional phase, and the time of resuming one's life, our efforts to assist young people will be enhanced. This will aid our revising and rebuilding teen lives.

Early or Initial Loss

The grief minister will note that initially the experience is one of shock, numbness, disbelief, or denial. These are some of the prevalent emotions. There is also anger, which may surface during this early time of grief. "How could God take away my father when I was so young?" "Why did God pick me rather than some of my friends who don't even love their parents?" Many questions arise and many are of a religious nature. The feelings of abandonment are very pronounced. The teenager truly feels lost. Life is devoid of meaning. There is this tremendous vacuum that no one seems to know how he or she is feeling.

Guilt is especially prevalent when there has been a lengthy illness. Teenagers may feel selfish because they did not spend more time with the dying loved one. They may feel guilty because they did not acknowledge that the dying was occurring. All the defenses and denials are now right in front of them and need to be addressed.

When we lose a loved one, part of ourselves dies. Teenagers feel this as well. In the teenager's world he or she must soon return to school. There they can become very self-conscious. It is very difficult to be the focal point of classmates due to grief. There may be the surfacing of hidden fears such as how they will now be seen by classmates and friends. Inappropriate questions and remarks can trigger a real sadness in the teenager's life. The grief minister and other professionals have to be aware of what the teenager is going through. If ever there is a need for a compassionate listener, it is for the teenager experiencing grief.[2] It is a unique challenge not only to be there during this critical time but also to know what the teen is experiencing and is not always able to communicate.

For teenagers, amid all their added complexities, the time span for making adjustments can be noticeably longer. Adults must be patient and understanding of how stressful grief is for teenagers. This is sometimes difficult to understand when there are few outward signs.

Teenagers, especially younger teens, are individual mixes of child and adult. As teens transition through childhood's end they do so at their own pace and schedule. Add to such a confusing state the feelings of loss, and it is very difficult to know how teens will react. Unless one takes the time to allow teens to reveal their feelings at their own pace, it can be difficult to assist them through grief. Teens, being that combination of child and adult, experience grief in both hemispheres; as children there may be "magical thinking" still involved in their minds. It might be something they did or did not do; as adults, teens can rationalize that it is not the case yet the feelings of guilt and sadness linger.

The maturity level will determine how grief is experienced and which aspect of the child/adult will dominate. For the consoling adult it is important that we allow teens permission to be who they are—children, adults, or a combination who are confused, hurt, and depressed. The good grief minister will not denigrate or characterize feelings as childish—they are emotions that are always legitimate.

Transitions/Changes/Adjusting

Most of us find after the numbing is worn off we have to accept and go through our grief. This is for many the most difficult part of the process. The body has almost anesthetized itself. Now we realize without the numbing that grief can be very difficult. For the teenager the question is, "Who can I share these feelings with?" Mistakenly our society thinks that after a few months we return to "normal." This view serves only to have teenagers suffer on their own and perhaps act out inappropriately. During the months necessary to accept and do the essential grieving of sorting out our emotions, there is a need more than ever for someone to be there. The more present we are without prying into the teenager's life, the more we actually help. This is truly a ministry of presence.

It is usually during the transitions when help is sought. The teenager realizes that he or she has to address this major loss.

We must look for ways to be comforting without taking away the grief. The last thing a teenager needs is to be rescued. Rescuing often consists of not giving the teenager necessary space to express real emotions. The teenager needs to be allowed to own his or her feelings.

Support groups for teenagers are more complex. It is not a good idea to have a support group facilitated by another teen. Somehow with bereavement support groups of peers, peer pressure could actually have everyone agree upon life to be seen as truly "empty" or "the pits." It is good facilitation when a grief minister assists the teens in admitting to the change and beginning to try to sort things out.

Religious faith is an all-important aspect of anyone's grief. The teenager needs to form a new relationship in faith with the deceased. Our gatherings with youth should not avoid praying for those who have died. We have to explain what a "continuing bond" means. Death is not the end of the relationship. Not including the losses, even early ones, on our journey only contributes to the denial. Our youth groups, Catholic schools, and parishes need to include grief as part of the faith journey.

Platitudes do not help the teenager to go through grief. It takes time to process the loss. To superimpose religious statements only generates resentment. Acceptance takes considerable time. Eventually the teenager will come to accept the loss and try to see it as part of God's plan. To say too soon that it is God's will only complicates matters.

Reorganizing/Readjusting

Another time of grief is that of reorganization. This means that the teenager is functioning fairly well and is once again at home with his or her feelings in society. This does not mean that the grief is over. We know there is no time limit for grieving. We adjust but we are not the same. It is important, especially during holidays and anniversaries, that the teenager be made aware of the ongoing nature of grief. The teenager has to be told grief does not completely end but we learn to manage it.

It takes a lifetime to sort out grief. Teenagers start earlier, and it is a long journey ahead of them. How well they do depends upon the support network and the degree of empathy we are willing to give. In our society teenagers are often excluded since we perceive them as still very young. Excluding them is a real mistake, especially when it comes to grief.

A grief minister's challenge is to include all who are grieving losses. The more grief ministers can make our congregations, schools, and society aware of loss throughout the life span, the better we become at reaching out and bringing healing. These are evangelizing moments.

Context of Faith/Regaining Trust

When we grieve we endure many changes. The grief minister is there to facilitate healthy change and more. Transformation is a key word for grief ministry. What has happened can spark religious faith. We need to help teenagers place their loss into the context of faith. They need spiritual guidance while they journey through grief. The moments of loss, the searching and yearning for the loved one, the feelings of abandonment can be placed into the context of faith. For grieving teenagers this is truly transformative when this happens.

We are called to be instruments of healing for teenagers. We must aid them in facing bereavement not alone but with the support of the believing community. Time spent with teens is time that assists them with acceptance and a more spiritual life.

Ministy Toolbox

1. Discuss the meaning of loss with a teenager.

2. Explore the spiritual dimensions of loss with a teenager.

3. Inquire about how well a young person is doing in managing loss.

4. Discuss with grief ministers what vehicles or places for healing exist for young people in your community.

5. Be aware that the term "digitally literate" applies to today's teen.

6. Cyberspace is a major contextual environment in which teens deal with grief. This entails instant messaging, texting, and social media. All are vehicles of communication, even about loss. This has been called "thanatechnology."

7. Rituals and art therapy are more than helpful.

8. Psalms are "icebreakers" for teens, facilitating in telling their story.

6

Grief Minister and Religious Expression

I lift up my eyes to the hills—
   from where will my help come?
My help comes from the LORD,
   who made heaven and earth. (Ps 121:1-2)

The crisis of separation and loss cries out for religious expression. Our communication with God is often paralyzed while we endure critical events. Our loss colors everything. How can I pray? Is this an experience that only I really feel? Will this mood ever change?

The grief minister will hear these questions while conversing with the bereaved. The preceding are questions of balance that often occur as we find ourselves totally out of step in our lives. Our prayer life appears to be in shambles. Chaos and confusion control our very being. Everything about ourselves screams for relief. Where does one turn when bad things happen? Is there an oar to help us steer when we feel ourselves at sea in a fog of loss?

There is the rich resource of the psalms to help us minister to those who are suffering from the loss of a loved one. The psalms are a powerful resource for coping with life's tragedies. The grief minister can help the bereaved to realize that by journeying into the psalms they allow us to explore new ways to express separation and loss. The psalms can be that oar that helps us steer through our grief. Psalms provide considerable meaning and management for times while we are grieving. They are a powerful resource for guidance.

The psalms of lament bring a dimension of meaning for the grief stricken not found anywhere else. Anger, feelings of abandonment, guilt, yearning to be with the loved one, and crying out for meaning are emotions that stimulate us to seek help. Very often the grief minister will note that the bereaved while grieving become confused about expressing feelings in the religious setting. They may find themselves gravitating toward others and yet still avoid talking about their loss.

Many grieving people do not know how to tell others about conflicts. They lock away their feelings of abandonment and anger. This is common when someone is angry with God for taking the deceased loved one. Somehow we have been conditioned to misinterpret their lack of crying out as a lack of faith. The psalms are a pastoral way that allows us to express our true feelings.

Rekindling Trust

We can describe the bereaved personality as lacking in confidence or trust. Loss often requires rebuilding lost trust or faith in life as meaningful and a place where there is happiness. Every aspect of life seems to shatter when significant loss occurs. The loss seems to infect our very lives, turning stable faith and hope into new losses. The losses appear to pile up one after another. There is a total disorganization and chaos. For the grief minister, relating to the bereaved entails helping piece together broken lives. This requires patience, presence, and empathy in a process that for many goes on for years. Again, there really is no time limit for grieving.

Mary, who is sixty-two years old, recently lost her thirty-year-old daughter. The daughter died very suddenly from a heart attack. Mary has always been a very prayerful person. Now she is withdrawn and tells only a few friends how she really feels. She is angry at God and feels he abandoned her.

The psalms can be of considerable assistance in comforting Mary. You can see the look of relief come over grieving people when certain psalms are prayed with them. If we take a few minutes to pray with those whose lives are shattered by loss, real healing occurs. The Scriptures in the psalms speak to critical situations of separation and loss. When you pray the following psalm allow your imagination to see yourself comforting others while conversing with God:

> *Psalm 130*
> Out of the depths I cry to you, O LORD.
>> LORD, hear my voice!
> Let your ears be attentive
>> to the voice of my supplications! (vv. 1-2)

The initial crying out of the supplicant illustrates a way to call upon the Lord. The psalms are truly a school of prayer. They teach us how to talk with God.

> If you, O LORD, should mark iniquities,
>> Lord, who could stand?
> But there is forgiveness with you,
>> so that you may be revered.
> I wait for the LORD, my soul waits
>> and in his word I hope. (vv. 3-5)

The psalms allow us not to deny what is really happening. Iniquity is part of life and our prayer life has to connect with what is really occurring. Accepting what is happening and still trusting in the Lord is experiencing an authentic faith response.

> [M]y soul waits for the Lord
>> more than those who watch for the morning,
>> more than those who watch for the morning.
> O Israel, hope in the LORD!
>> For with the LORD there is steadfast love,
>> and with him is great power to redeem.
> It is he who will redeem Israel
>> from all its iniquities. (vv. 6-8)

Among all the characteristics of grief, longing is one of the most prevalent. Our souls yearn for fulfillment. We yearn to be with those who have died. This longing is often expressed by searching and even revisiting places that both the bereaved and the deceased frequented in life. The psalm places our yearning into the context of redemptive trust in the Lord.

There are other psalms that are appropriate for conversing with God. We are all familiar with Psalm 23. This exceptional psalm sets the tone for coping with loss. So clearly does it express inner feelings that it has become the psalm for grief and guidance. When we experience loss there is need for guidance "through the dark valley." The metaphor of the Lord as our Shepherd is a helping metaphor, especially when we feel aimless and confused. We turn to the psalms to process our feelings in a purposeful manner. Our emotions may be chaotic when grief enters our lives.

Anger is a strange emotion in our culture. While its extremes are glorified in movies and television, in reality anger is generated by feelings of hopelessness and loss, and when it is not correctly channeled as an emotion it is very destructive. Consequently for many who associate feelings of anger with the overall cultural denial, it is very difficult to know what is appropriate behavior. Some highlights from the following psalm relate to anger. This psalm not only reveals our real feelings but puts them into a healing context through prayer:

> *Psalm 22*
> My God, my God, why have you forsaken me?
>> Why are you so far from helping me, from the words of
>>> my groaning?
> O my God, I cry by day, but you do not answer;
>> and by night, but find no rest. . . .
> Do not be far from me,
>> for trouble is near
>> and there is no one to help.

When we examine Psalm 22 we are struck by the strong emotion of asking why, yet in the demanding there is also a rekindling of trust. There is a change of mood and a seeking of strength. This is a channeling of the anger by actually conversing with God. The psalms give us permission to be ourselves in our prayer life. When we pray the psalms, we do not pretend or camouflage our feelings.

When we help the bereaved to identify with the psalmist's anger, feelings of loss, and crying out, it connects us with a deeper spiritual reality. The bereaved are empowered to own their feelings. At the same time these feelings are not thought to be immoral or abnormal. They are an entirely understandable human response to loss. Grief is put into the context of something that has to be gone through with the hope of managing the loss. This means taking the risk of trusting and loving again after one of life's hurts.

Journeying through Grief

Crisis counselors tell us that the sooner we express our losses, the better we go through grief. When we delay such expression, we pay a big price. Physical and emotional difficulties may result when we suppress our emotions.

We are given through the psalms a wonderful resource in faith. In keeping with revelation, we are given insights about the mystery of life. Through God's self-communication we are empowered to cope with our loss while we journey toward the kingdom. The psalms should be viewed as nourishment and a map for that journey. Reading and eventually praying the psalms can unlock emotions of grief so we can traverse on the journey.

Prayer of the Church

The psalms are the expression of faith in the *Order of Christian Funerals* within the section on the Office of the Dead. An important option in the ritual is to celebrate the Office at the time of the vigil. The prayer of the church connects us with the entire Body of Christ, especially during grief.

"The community's celebration of the hours acknowledges that spiritual bond that links the Church on earth with the Church in heaven, for it is in union with the whole Church that this prayer is offered on behalf of the deceased" (*Order of Christian Funerals* 349). This spiritualizes our continual bonds.

Coming together as family and community during an intense period of loss can be extremely beneficial. Keeping the hours acknowledges that the whole church stands with the bereaved as they strain to catch a glimpse of eternity and God's love for us. A more detailed treatment of the psalms and prayer are given in my book *Challenging the Landscape of Loss*[1] (chap. 9: "Expressing Ourselves Through Prayer").

In Imitation of Christ

Through praying the psalms assemblies in faith pray in Jesus' voice (*Order of Christian Funerals* 355). Jesus prayed the psalms during his life on earth. In imitation of Jesus we learn how to empty ourselves to the Father and find real life by doing so. Just as Jesus cried out using the psalms at his crucifixion, so too we are empowered to cry out. When we cry out using the thoughts of the psalmist, we too grow in our hope for eternal life.

Ministry Toolbox

Bereavement Exercises and Reflections

1. Recognize the psalms as a resource for healing.
2. The psalms help us to express our innermost feelings while grieving. What feelings or thoughts are unlocked for you by the psalms?
3. How do the psalms assist you in your journey through grief?
4. Can you accept your loss better by praying the psalms?
5. In light of your life's journey, compose a suitable psalm.
6. Find a quiet place and meditate on your favorite psalm.

7

Grief Minister and Anniversary Effect

[A]nd so we will be with the Lord forever. Therefore encourage one another with these words. (1 Thess 4:17-18)

Every parish has to be sensitive to needs facing their congregations. There are times when certain members are very much in need of ministry. The grief minister is a key person for recognizing these critical times for the bereaved. As a grief minister you are also a "crisis minister." As a crisis minister you are sensitive to certain events, occasions, and times that affect those who are suffering from grief. It is necessary that the grief minister possess an awareness of how to address and help meet special needs of the bereaved.

The grief minister is one who must realize that not everyone looks forward to happiness in the holidays. For many, it is a time of great joy but also a season of sorrow. Even those who are not actively grieving are very likely to feel a mixture of emotions. Happiness may be tinted with a sense of loss and sad memories. It is a time of reflection on past holidays and the times of our lives without very important people who have left us. When the tinges of sadness begin to color our anticipation of the holiday, the reflective sadness becomes greater. If this happens, the grief minister may assess the person as suffering from "anniversary effect."

Anniversary effect touches all of us at one time or another. The longer we live, the more losses we have to experience. Holidays and holy days recall happiness since our earliest childhood. Many of these memories cannot be reenacted. The landscape of memories are peopled by loved ones who have gone.[1]

The looks of joy and surprise when the right present was under the Christmas tree takes place in our bright memories of childhood. The laughter and merriment of that family gathering is impossible to happen again. Brothers, sisters, parents, husbands, wives, and even children have since died. How can we really be happy without them? Is there any sense in celebrating?

Grief Ministry during Holidays and Anniversaries

Grief ministers are challenged to be effective ministers during holidays and anniversaries. They need to be prepared to minister to those who, with feelings of loss, are emotionally more vulnerable than usual. Ministers, in ministering to others, have to be willing to do a self-evaluation on how they themselves are doing during holidays.

In ministry it is important to recall that we may experience many intense memories. Ministers are not immune to the suffering affecting those to whom they are ministering. Some have become friends with families over the years. All the more reason for grief ministers to be aware of having a supportive network.

Feelings of loss during anniversaries confirm the fact that there really is no time limit to grieving even if the loss is related to a Christmas even ten or twenty years ago. We learn to cope with grief; we never "get over it" or forget. The intensity of a grieving moment or event can dim the nicest of memories. The challenge is to be ever vigilant to put the loss into a context when we experience flashbacks from past losses. A certain song or familiar smell makes us recall the past losses. Many people experience such emotions with deep intensity.

There are continual feelings of sadness for the bereaved during anniversaries. Grief ministers tell us how difficult the holidays are especially for those who are experiencing a recent loss. The first years are certainly the most difficult. There are the constant reminders that life is different. The empty chair and the lack of a presence around the house are most noticeable. The compelling question for the bereaved is, "How can I survive this? How can this holiday ever mean anything more for me?"

Normal Anniversary Reactions

The grief minister has to bear in mind that for the most part anniversary reactions are normal. Reactions are telling examples of how the grieving process is progressing from recent losses. Keeping a calendar for ministry to the bereaved is very important in order to keep track of when anniversaries will be occurring. In this way the grief minister may schedule a pastoral visit with the still grieving parishioner at a time of heightened awareness. While it is a difficult time, it can also be a "graced" moment. With a little intervention in the form of a visit, it can make a huge difference in a person's life and the ability to continue.

Some of the following aspects of anniversary reactions among the bereaved may be noted:

- As the anniversary approaches, the bereaved may confide that there has been an increase in memories; often dreams increase, and other thoughts and feelings surface that they thought were long gone. They may once again think the "lost" loved one is nearby.

- The reemergence of emotions and thoughts associated with grief may appear. This can be alarming for the bereaved as they may think they are reliving and restarting the grieving process once again. Assurance that they are not going back to square one is very helpful.

- Avoidance may occur, which is a form of denial. The bereaved want to ignore events and memories that may remind them of their grief. They do not want to celebrate holidays. They feel safer if all days are uniform.

- The bereaved may not realize that they need to "sort out" how they will react on the upcoming date or anniversary.

The grief minister assists the parish by monitoring the impact anniversaries have on the bereaved. The scheduling of parish and family prayer services greatly assists the bereaved in acknowledging their loss. At the same time it assists them in owning their feelings and placing them into a religious context.[2]

Rituals are very important for coping with our emotions during anniversary reactions. They release our feelings and help us to acknowledge that the event is really happening. Rituals may be formal (in church) or informal (at home) and consist of activities that place the loss into the broader Christian context.

The grief minister should always be aware that the bereaved are more than often grieving as a family. During bereavement the family loses its equilibrium or balance. They are in need of adjustments. A family remembrance addresses the family as a system made up of grieving members.

Specific Anniversaries

During the first year after the death of a loved one certain anniversaries are more significant than others. If we look briefly at some of the major anniversaries and their implications for ministry to the bereaved, we will be better prepared to face the day when it arrives.

Celebrating the "month's mind Mass." Approximately a month after the funeral of a loved one there may be scheduled a special Mass. This Mass is for the intention of the loved one's salvation. Families who may still be shocked and numbed participate in the liturgy. The participation and ministry offered at this time are healing for families seeking ways to find meaning early on in their bereavement.

Planning the one-year anniversary. This first anniversary of death may be very difficult in the days and weeks before it takes place. The grief minister, in keeping in contact with the bereaved, may notice that the bereaved are under pressure but not know why. In discussing this first year, some important advice may be given to the bereaved. While talking with the bereaved, the grief minister may suggest that they carefully prepare for the anniversary and make plans for the day of the anniversary. The minister may remind them that often families get caught up with their lives and forget that the anniversary is about to happen. The day does not have to be something to avoid or dread. Instead, the bereaved can manage the grief better by trying to creatively respond rather than reacting.

The first anniversary is a time for the grief minister to make an assessment of how effective the ministry has been with the bereaved. It is more than appropriate to suggest to the bereaved that they do certain things at this time during bereavement. For example, if they are keeping a journal, they may want to do a review. They can look back and see how they have done in order to welcome the future.

The pastoral visit to the bereaved during what could be a most troublesome time makes all the difference. The grief minister is there to reassure and bring comforting ideas for how to go through the day. The role of the grief minister is very evident when the bereaved confide that they are new to the area. If they are trying to work through the loss in an unfamiliar setting, the church may act as a bridge. The bereaved, through the familiarity they have with faith, may adjust easier through spiritual suggestions. It also is recommended that the bereaved either visit or talk with friends from the area where they used to live.[3]

The eighteen-month point. Just when everyone thinks that the grief is over, the year-and-a-half point happens. It may seem that everything is back to "normal." Suddenly the bereaved may be surprised by a return of many of the initial feelings of loss. This may lead them to believe that they have really returned to square one. The grief minister is there to explain that this is a legitimate part of the grieving process. During bereavement we are still sorting things out after a year and a half. Once again this demonstrates that we cannot set time limits for bereavement. As another year goes by it will be evident to the bereaved that they are not struggling anywhere near as much as previously. It is more manageable.

After two years. It is very difficult for the bereaved to accept that they need to "move on." They have to be told that we go forward with our enduring bond. The two-year point often has with it some bittersweet realizations. The bereaved feel better and recognize the challenge that they have to go on with their lives. At the same time there are possible "misplaced" feelings of being disloyal to the loved one who has died. This is clearly present when a widow or widower has met someone who means a lot to him or her.[4] We cannot "police" the widow/widower about a new relationship. There is certainly no setting time limits for them.

The two-year point as an anniversary or marker point in the bereavement process brings with it many mixed feelings that need to be sorted out. The bereaved need to be assured that there is someone willing to listen to them. This can be very helpful for them and their family no matter what the new circumstances are.

Grief Reactions during Anniversaries

Grief ministers play a very significant part in the life of any community. They engage the bereaved in ways to ritualize and accept loss in their lives. They are catalysts for change and healing.

The grief minister should be familiar with intense grief reactions—especially on anniversaries within bereavement. The feelings of exhaustion, anxiety, inability to sleep well, loss of appetite, and even a return to shock and numbness are among the possible realities the minister now helps the bereaved to cope with. The grief minister explains that this is not a return to the beginning but a transitory aspect of "anniversary effect."

In many ways the only person really noting how someone is doing after two years may well be the grief minister. Everyone else is either too busy or preoccupied with other concerns in their lives. The grief minister is the one who is there for the bereaved to assure them that they will go through this period. They can explain "anniversary reactions."

Very often anniversaries tell us about ourselves. We experience self-discovery as we reexplore the meaning of our relationship with our loved ones who have died. They have lived their journey and we are still journeying. What we may discover is how well or poorly we did with our loved ones at the end of their lives.

The bereaved may find themselves during anniversaries with a need to verbalize feelings of emptiness and loss due to their thoughts about how they may have inadequately responded to the needs of a dying loved one. They may well be seeking forgiveness for not being there. These regrets and guilt can be overwhelming and may impede the grieving process.

Death takes many of us by surprise as we did not allow for such an eventuality. The grief minister has to stress a spirituality of an "enduring bond" with loved ones and trusting in God. It may be obvious to the grief minister that the level of faith maturity of a bereaved person may be lacking by not accepting the will of God. After a length of time the acceptance of the event and God's will is necessary for good grief.

Conversations with the bereaved may open up all of the emotions we associate with grief. The grief minister who enters into the bereavement of others has to be prepared for such realities. It is the grief minister who often stands alone in the community as the one willing to be with the bereaved.

The grief minister is called upon to utilize listening skills with the bereaved during anniversaries. This important skill is often overlooked or forgotten by those who merely "check in" and see how the bereaved are doing. It is important that the minister give the bereaved sufficient time during a visit to recollect or tell their loss story. Be open to sitting and visiting over tea or coffee. Allow the bereaved this "ritual" to prepare to talk with you. The ritual may be having tea or coffee or saying a short prayer. Grief ministers need to enter into the bereaved's world and allow them the opportunity to converse about the loss, whether it has been six months or six years or even more.

Offering Encouragement

It is the grief minister who encourages those who are grieving to participate in special anniversary activities. This contributes to shaping grief in ways that are healing and allow for better ways to cope. At the same time participation means preparing oneself ahead of time regarding how to participate and to what degree participation is possible.

As Christians the participation ought to include some way of making the day spiritual. A spiritual celebration activates rich resources in faith. Our ability to trust and love again are highlighted through liturgical celebrations. These celebrations help us to remember our loved ones and offer love through worshiping in hope for the kingdom of God.

A faith-filled practice is the memorial eucharistic celebration. To see a family come together and remember a loved one on certain anniversaries puts everything into perspective. The family begins what may be one of the most difficult days of the year with the rich resource of liturgy. At the same time it illustrates a family's faith response.

After the memorial liturgy families gather for breakfast. Some families plan a special event that helps them to stay together for the day. This may be visiting a museum, some historic place, or having a family meal. It may mean going to some place that always has been significant in the family's tradition.

With the help of grief ministers the bereaved can plan ahead and find some real peace. Grief ministers act as an instrument of healing. The bereaved benefit from their presence at the often critical and overlooked time of anniversaries. Ministry at this time is an essential expression of ministry to the bereaved.

Ministry means being with people. This is especially true for grief ministry when people are in crisis. Serving the bereaved during critical moments such as anniversaries has lasting effects. The grief minister is acting as a compassionate companion to those who are in need of the community's supportive presence.

Ministry Toolbox

Try to remember significant dates for the bereaved in your ministry.

Explain what "anniversary effect" means for that day.

Reassure the bereaved they are not returning to step one in their grief.

Provide spiritual ideas and actions (which give meaning) for the day.

8

Grief Minister and Journal Writing

[H]ope does not disappoint us, because God's love has been poured into our hearts through the Holy Spirit that has been given to us. (Rom 5:5)

When I was in graduate school a major professor used to describe himself in ministry as a "player coach." It is amazing after all these years what remarks and insights stay with you. As erudite as he was, the professor knew how to describe what it meant to be with people in their lives. His words aptly describe the way the grief minister enters into the lives of the bereaved when he or she helps them with the healing venture of keeping a journal. It is a privilege to participate and offer coaching to those who want to give some meaning to their loss through journal writing. In many ways we are co-constructing with them as they rebuild their lives.

Everyone's journey through grief is unique. How well or, for that matter, how poorly we progress depends on our ability to be creative in our grief responses. Our personal responses are colored by many factors. Among the factors are the bond we have with our loved ones, our history of past losses, the circumstances surrounding the loss, as well as other issues such as health and age.

Creative journaling also serves as a tool for healing our many hurts. We literally step outside of ourselves when we write our way through some very difficult days. When the grief minister suggests that journal writing is a positive way to go through difficult days, considerable healing can occur.

Ministry and Communicating

Grief ministers do a real service for the bereaved when they advise them about what grief can do. They can communicate to the bereaved that if they allow it to happen, grief can control and overwhelm their lives. It is far better to manage losses rather than have our losses so color our lives that grief becomes our manager. Managing our losses entails doing important actions that help us to accept and define what is occuring in our life.

Grief response includes the necessity of rituals. We need to express ourselves through signs and symbols. Ritual gestures and actions connect us with our loss while allowing us to manage it in healing ways. Through our rituals we put our loss into context and redefine it, making it manageable for us in most difficult times.

Journal writing includes all the elements of a ritual for our necessary response to loss. When we write about ourselves and our thoughts and feelings, we utilize symbols and gestures. We turn the art of writing and reflecting into a ritual. Making the commitment to "journal" imposes parameters for our grief. The commitment—daily reflecting and writing—is repetitive, which imposes a ritualistic structure on us, especially if we set aside a certain time to do so. The best journal writers usually have a set time and place to reflect and write each day. Having this structure imposes order amid the turmoil and confusion and gives meaning when we accept our losses.

While we write we reflect on loss and are able to step back from intense feelings, making them manageable within the confines of the text we're writing. Writing about our losses helps us to forgo those barriers and the chains that bind us to our loss.

Spiritual Dimensions

The presence of the grief minister is a reminder to the bereaved that there is the spiritual dimension for our grief. The grief minister reminds us that along with the physical and emotional expressions accompanying loss is the simultaneous need for spiritual expression. Journal writing is a way to express our innermost feelings. It is a suitable way to help ourselves and very often to honor the memory of our loved one who has died. It furthers the way we maintain our enduring bond.

During times of loss the spiritual action that confronts us is relinquishing the physical relationship and welcoming a new way of spiritually relating. This all-important action may literally test our faith. While we grieve our faith and belief may well be troubled. As we journey through grief our journaling can be a valuable tool for healing our brokenness in both the present and future. The new understanding about continual bonds reinforces our faith and love for those who have died. Our calling upon the Holy Spirit inspires us.

Resources in Faith

The grief minister helps the bereaved with a good idea that before we begin writing our journal, we do some "scriptural homework." The Scriptures are filled with images and healing ways to manage our losses.

When we meditate on certain psalms we receive healing interventions from our loving God who shows us ways to arrange our thoughts for effective healing through journal writing. We need ways to organize what may be the chaos that surrounds us while we grieve. Our very thoughts about what is occurring need some structuring. The psalms help us to sort out what is happening and provide ways to express and manage our loss.

In this ministry to the bereaved, we can easily see ourselves opening up a Bible with the bereaved. Together we can review certain psalms that speak to the grieving process and serve as entry headings for our grief journals. Often the grief stricken will choose a psalm quote as an entry and catalyst for thoughts to write about.

Feelings of Loss

We may have feelings of abandonment, guilt, emptiness, anger, and yearning to be with our loved one. We are gifted with psalms that bring healing and are a catalyst as we fashion and shape our grief journals.[1] Initially Psalm 130 speaks to our loss:

> Out of the depths I cry to you, O LORD;
>> Lord, hear my voice!
> Let your ears be attentive
>> to the voice of my supplications! (Ps 130:1-2)

Searching for Guidance

Writing a journal in the context of faith requires our *surrendering* to the Lord for guidance. Psalm 23 provides us with the healing image of the Lord as our Shepherd:

> The LORD is my shepherd; I shall not want.
>> He makes me lie down in green pastures;
> he leads me beside still waters;
>> he restores my soul. (Ps 23:1-3)

Feelings of Abandonment

The psalm writer is very aware of what constitutes loss. Reading Psalm 22 speaks to our feelings of isolation and abandonment:

> My God, my God, why have you forsaken me?
>> Why are you so far from helping me, from the words of my
>>> groaning?
> O my God, I cry by day, but you do not answer;
>> and by night, but find no rest.
>
> Yet you are holy,
>> enthroned on the praises of Israel.

In you our ancestors trusted;
    they trusted, and you delivered them.
To you they cried, and were saved;
    in you they trusted, and were not put to shame. (Ps 22:1-5)

When Grief Is Yearning

Our lives are so very different that we yearn for previous experiences of being with our loved ones. Psalm 42 helps us to place these emotions into the context of faith:

As a deer longs for flowing streams,
    so my soul longs for you, O God.
My soul thirsts for God,
    for the living God.
When shall I come and behold
    the face of God?
My tears have been my food
    day and night,
while people say to me continually,
    "Where is your God?"

These things I remember,
    as I pour out my soul. (Ps 42:1-4)

Longing for Freedom

We live and wonder about our experience of loss. Grief sets no time limits. Our grief changes as our lives continue. Yet we still persist in crying out, "How long, O LORD?" Psalm 13 verbalizes our human cries about the duration of loss. This psalm is again another catalyst for thought as we live and write about our losses:

How long, O LORD? Will you forget me forever?
    How long will you hide your face from me?
How long must I bear pain in my soul,
    and have sorrow in my heart all day long?
How long shall my enemy be exalted over me?

Consider and answer me, O LORD my God! (Ps 13:1-3)

Stress Reduction

As grief ministers we can reassure the bereaved that journal writing does not have to be a literary masterpiece. In fact it really does not even have to follow literary rules. What is most important is to keep in mind why we are writing. It is not for publication. Rather, it is meant to bring healing and restore our sense of balance during a critical time in our life.

It is good to emphasize with the bereaved that while we grieve we need to tell and retell our story of loss. This is of great assistance in another primary concern for grief—the *acceptance* of the loss. We begin to become more reality-based in accepting that our loved one has really died. While we put our thoughts and feelings down on paper or visualize them on a computer screen, stress is reduced. Studies have shown that there is stress reduction when we write about what has happened to us and how we relate to our emotions. In addressing stresses we reduce that stress.

Our emotional well-being is enhanced by simply writing in our journal for a brief time each day. The time spent does not have to be lengthy. It may be as short as ten to twenty minutes or even less per day. Our actual time writing may be preceded by briefly exploring God's word. As previously noted, making the psalms our own is good grief as well as good prayer.

Structuring Our Grief

In grief ministry it is good to acknowledge for the bereaved that during bereavement we may enter a chaotic period. Our physical, emotional, and spiritual health is often in turmoil. We need relief and often cry out for ways to give some form or structure to our lives. Remembering again that "one size does not fit all," we have to relate as well to a bereaved person who is peaceful because a loved one is not suffering any longer.

Journal writing structures these painful and accepting emotions. We step outside of ourselves and express those thoughts and feelings in written form. Through describing our innermost emotions and thoughts, we feel relief from those stresses.

Self-Discovery

Grief can radically change our worldview. Our experience is so intense we often feel as if time has frozen. How can life continue when everything has stopped? Memories, dreams, and reflections about our loved one are more vivid than ever. The past and frozen present rule our lives.

You may want to relate to the bereaved how the spiritual writer Henri Nouwen found writing about his mother's death as personal expression and vehicle for his grief. Shortly after his mother's death he wrote to his father *A Letter of Consolation*. He wrote the letter for himself as well as his father. He states in the introduction about how he needed to "listen to my own inner cries." The value of writing about grief is again stated when he wrote, "Once I started to write I realized how much I felt, how much I wanted to say, and how much had remained hidden during the six months since mother had died."[2]

The psychology of loss tells us that in death our loved ones are more present to us than even while alive. The way we manage our losses tells how well or poorly we do and provides us insights about ourselves. We experience significant aspects of our personality. Everything may be brought out in raw relief.

Journal writing encourages better living. We begin journaling when we are ready, and we are urged to begin when there is a need and not wait for the problem to overwhelm us and become the driving force in our lives. This can lead us to self-discovery. We are changing, and through our journaling we can write about who we are really becoming in our bereavement.

The Writing Experience

Becoming aware helps our writing. The flow of ideas and the writing need to be fueled. Our personal story needs to be stated and restated many times over.[3]

Getting Started

Once grief ministers have examined some compelling reasons for journal writing, they can in a practical way help the bereaved to get started. They can assure them that the actual nuts and bolts of putting together a journal is not all that difficult.

1. *Select for yourself the right notebook.* This selection may range from a three-ring binder to a computer journal formatted according to your likes.

2. *You may want to include art or poetry or photos of the loved one.* Art expresses ways to dialogue about loss. Certain music, art, and poetry capture special remembrances about our loved one. Photos of loved ones can serve as a catalyst for recalling memories of shared times that are now put into a new context.

3. *Write at a time that is best for you.* It is helpful to select a time of day when you can give fifteen or twenty minutes without interruptions. Don't worry about the length of the entry.

4. *Let your writing flow.* When we open thoughts according to our stream of consciousness, we are by far in a more conducive state of mind for healing revelations. Spiritual unveiling occurs and helps us to experience healing images in our mind. This leads to imaginative writing. Imagination and healing go hand in hand.

5. *Write about fulfilled and unfulfilled dreams and hopes.* When we write about a loved one who has died, many thoughts come to mind. Our loss may well be the death of a dream connected to a loved one's life—our work with him or her, partnership in life's ventures, and other dreams fulfilled or vanquished.

6. *Remember in grief you are sorting things out.* While we grieve we have to decide what memories and dreams we will hold onto and what we will forgo. Writing helps us sort everything out.

7. *Focus on how grief is a time for self-discovery.* All of us go through changes and transformations as we go through life's passages. Documenting our changes helps us as we see ourselves in the present and helps chart our future course.

These are a few suggestions to help the bereaved get started on what may be one of the most important journeys of their life. Journal writing is a healing tool that will bring tears and joy. You may want to conclude your time with the bereaved with a suggestion that they begin their writing with a short prayer. An even better way is to pray a prayer with them for journal writing.

Ministry Toolbox

A Journal Writing Prayer

O Lord, I ask you to direct my writing as I write about my grief.

Help me to realize that you will inspire me with healing and hope as I recall so very much.

In your kindness I ask you to open up new ways of relating to my loved one [mention name] and give me the strength to continue this in my own life's journey. Amen.

Grief Minister and
Liturgy Preparation

If you direct your heart rightly,
  you will stretch out your hands toward him. (Job 11:13)

Liturgy preparation is an aspect we do not want to overlook when we consider grief ministry. Preparing for the funeral of a loved one is an essential concern for the grief minister. The grief minister is the one who meets with bereaved family members to plan the funeral liturgy. This is a critical moment that often sets the tone for the bereaved throughout the grieving process.

Families need this ministry in order to worship meaningfully at the funeral Mass. The grief minister has to keep in mind that the funeral is the introduction to mourning. It is a significant moment for ministry that colors the expression of grief in the context of faith. During this time of great need the grief minister is a key person in assisting the bereaved in preparing their hearts for worship.

Paul Irion, in his work on funerals and bereavement, gives us the following valuable insight as to the importance of ministry at this time:

The funeral itself is only one part, sometimes even a small part, in the whole psychological process of meeting bereavement. Yet, because of its public nature it is extremely important. It represents the response of the community or the church to the

emotional experience of the mourners. Thus, it cannot be re-
garded as either irrelevant or contradictory to the psychological
process of acceptance, release, expression and assimilation that
enable the mourner to endure and overcome the tremendous
disorganization of his life which has taken place.[1]

Grief Minister's Role

It cannot be overemphasized how important the grief minister
is in meeting with families. Liturgy preparation is far more than
just the assigning of roles. While choosing the lectors and gift
bearers is important for the liturgy, it cannot be the principal
concern. More important is the family's acceptance of the need
for a funeral and placing their loss into the faith context.

The celebration of the funeral has many purposes. Among
the purposes for a funeral are the following: (1) The ritual and
prayers are for the deceased and a sign of our respect and hope
for salvation for both the deceased and ourselves. (2) Prayers
are also offered for those who mourn. Their hearts find comfort
through placing their loss into the context of faith and trust in
God. (3) The funeral symbols and ritual actions connect us with
the eternal and remind us that we are witnessing the completion of the deceased's journey in this world. We are helping the
deceased to cross over the waters of death into the reign of God.

The grief minister has to be aware that in our society we are
accustomed to thinking of the bereaved as those being cared
for by others during the funeral. Some would even assign a
victim mentality to the bereaved. In this way of thinking the
idea is to do everything for them. They should not be asked to
decide anything. This is not an accurate picture. Even though
the bereaved are facing many thoughts and feelings, they too
are being called to minister and participate.

Families and friends must minister to each other. The grief
minister may act as a catalyst for ministry within the bereaved
family. As a grief minister there is the need to remind the family to think in terms of family and cherish one another. The
minister may remind the families about those who are excluded

while they grieve. This is especially evident when families do not include children. Among the elderly very often the aged deceased's siblings are overlooked in their grief.

Ministry and participation in the funeral are not passive endeavors. Rather, real love and compassion are expressed within families when they foster healing and hope to each other and the entire family unit.

The grief minister, in meeting with the bereaved, alleviates considerable anxiety. It may have been years since the family had a funeral. They do not know what to expect. Another scenario is that the family is not all that religious. This is a moment to be present and understanding, helping them to be familiar with the importance of worship. The words given in helping them, in God's grace, will go far beyond the time of the funeral. Again the consoling grief minister is a person of faith who is empathic and caring. True evangelizing occurs.

Ritual Awareness

Grief ministers prepare themselves for meeting with bereaved families for liturgical preparation by becoming familiar with the importance of ritual. When grief ministers have a good appreciation of what rituals accomplish, they find themselves far more effective in communicating with the bereaved. Rituals have a very valuable and healing role with those who are suffering a loss. Through rituals we are aided in adjusting to loss. Ritual gestures and actions along with symbols greatly influence the grieving process. When the bereaved participate in rituals, they are becoming aware of the need to express their innermost emotions utilizing words and gestures as vehicles.

We noted in the chapter on journal writing that, according to Henri Nouwen, we need to visit the place of our own powerlessness. The experience of loss in death can make us feel helpless. We are off balance and our physical, emotional, and spiritual life yearns for stability. Through rituals we enact in healthy and healing ways how we really feel during a critical time in our lives.

Rituals connect us with our own scattered and often frag-
mented feelings. At the same time they assist us in accepting
the reality of our losses. They help us to overcome practicing
avoidance and denial of losses. Being present and engaging,
ritual draws us into the faith embrace where losses are put into
the larger perspective. Our outlook is changed.

Pastoral Scenario

The following pastoral scenario illustrates the possible setting
for meeting with families in order to prepare the funeral liturgy.

Maura, as a parish grief minister, made an appointment to
meet with the Jones family at 1:00 p.m. in the parish center office. There are a number of ministers in the parish ministry of
consolation. Maura's role is to assist the bereaved in preparing the
funeral Mass. She is familiar with all of the moments or stations
as they are put forth in the *Order of Christian Funerals*. The family was primarily concerned about what to do during the Mass.

When Maura entered the parish office, she saw two familiar
faces. There were four people waiting for her. It was the family
of Mr. Jones, who had been one of Maura's Communion visita-
tions. Maura had visited Mr. Jones throughout his illness and was
with him when hospice workers were there at the end of a very
lengthy illness. It was fortunate that she already knew the family.
After some brief introductions and words of condolence to the
other relatives, she made some remarks as to how important the
liturgy is for everyone. The family responded, expressing their
wishes. Maura was very aware of the circumstances of the death
and this helped her in making preparations.

Maura easily explained that, according to our Catholic ritual,
there are many options and ways for families to participate and
minister. The family responded with interest and questions about
how to approach the actual funeral.

Maura, as a grief minister, gave a very fine presentation that
served as an overview to the ritual. She communicated to the
bereaved that when we think of the funeral as the completion of

the journey begun in baptism, then everything is much easier to appreciate and understand. The liturgy itself teaches and instills a deep realization that the death of a Christian is a sacred time for all.

Maura explained that the symbols associated with baptism illustrate during the liturgy how the gathering together of the family and friends completes the deceased's earthly journey. The use of the white pall on the casket along with holy water symbolizes the white garment and holy water during baptism. The Easter candle gives hope in the resurrection. As we died to sin and rose in hope in baptism, now we recall this as the earthly journey ends. The signs, symbols, and rituals that were interwoven throughout our faith life now come together to complete the tapestry of a Christian life. Sacred signs, symbols, and images send significant messages of faith to the assembly. They help us to experience the spiritual transformations so necessary for spiritual acceptance of loss.

Maura gave the family a consoling thought as a grief minister about the liturgy. She told them that so many years ago when the deceased was an infant he was carried into the assembly of faith by relatives and friends. Now in death his body is once again carried into the church by this generation of family and friends to pray for him that he will go forth to the kingdom of heaven.

Such images give added emphasis and consolation to those asked to participate in the ritual. Those invited to the ministry of pallbearers to carry the deceased Christian into the church should be reminded of the importance of this role. The family in the gathering area places the while pall over the casket. A hymn of hope is sung as the procession takes place. Even though there are tears in our eyes, they do not obscure the symbols of hope and a vision of eternal life for our loved one when we will once again be with him or her.

Liturgical Consolation

As the grief minister, Maura communicates to the family the rich resource of faith evident in the Catholic funeral ritual. The consoling images given in the sacred readings from both the

Hebrew Scriptures and the New Testament readings are high-lighted in preparing liturgy. Parish ministers may use the ritual *Order of Christian Funerals* or my *Planning the Catholic Funeral.* It is consoling for families to request that a family member or a friend of the family proclaim the readings during the funeral Mass. The options are spelled out in the planning guide. Before this happens, the grief minister who is preparing with them needs to give some brief instruction about the lector's ministry. Such a catechesis or instruction will greatly assist a lector, especially if he or she is from another parish.

It is important for Maura, in talking with the family about selecting a lector, that she keep in mind that being a lector entails more than just reading in church. A lector is a minister to the assembly and is there to minister to the community. In the instance of a funeral Mass there are basic needs facing the assembly. The lector is serving the assembly of faith when he or she proclaims the Scriptures in a consoling way. This means that there has to be an awareness of the consoling and hopeful themes put forth in the Scriptures surrounding the death of a Christian. Selecting a lector recommended by the family prompts a certain question. "Has the person been a lector before in church? Will he or she be able to handle this duty?" Liturgy planning is far more than only the assigning of roles.

There are other options available for participation by the family. The presentation of gifts at the offertory may be done by family members. It is during the presentation of gifts that we have seen grandchildren and other young relatives participate in traditional and unique ways. Young children may be allowed to bring up a drawing or other small memento for placement at the foot of the altar.

When meeting with families the grief minister has to approach the "Farewell Remembrance" during the final commendation and farewell in the funeral carefully. There are developing opinions as to what is the best time to remember the deceased Christian. Some parishes and dioceses have decided that a more appropriate time is during the vigil. The grief minister with the parish staff has to be clear about what policy will be held by their parish or diocese. Since the promulgation of the new ritual in 1989, the "farewell" along with what is appropriate music have been issues that need to be addressed. In my opinion both of these issues relate to how people appreciate or do not appreciate the sacred nature of liturgy. While it is very understandable that emotions while grieving are very intense, there does have to be an order and sacred way of celebrating funeral Masses. Usually there are not difficulties with those who are members of the worshiping community. I have found most of the problems arise in our secular society with those who are "unchurched" and are not familiar with the need for liturgical guidelines from dioceses and parishes.

One of the more difficult concerns facing grief ministers is the "farewell." In many ways it has become part of the culture that holds to the importance of a eulogy. For the secular society a eulogy usually consists of fond memories, some humorous stories about what a great person the deceased was. A "remembrance" in the context of the Catholic ritual is a recollection of the deceased life in the spirit. It is always done in the faith context and really focuses on the faith legacy the deceased gives us. If a person had been dedicated to helping the poor at a soup kitchen, then the remembrance might focus on how the deceased lived out the beatitudes through his or her service and how this dedication challenges us to do the same.

Eulogies are not part of the Catholic tradition. We believe that we are saved not by our own merits but only through Christ. Consequently we remember the deceased Christian in the context of faith. We praise God for the gifts given to the Christian during his or her earthly life. This emphasis is an expression of trust in God in whom we live and breathe and have our being. All praise must be given to the One who gives life and inspires all that we say and do. "Only our good deeds go with us."[2]

Being with the bereaved is a time of evangelization. Those who have been aware in practicing their faith for years now have an opportunity to experience consolation. The grief minister is the evangelizer. The grief minister can present themes of hope that will cooperate with the working of the Holy Spirit touching the bereaved's lives while they mourn.

Grief ministers are with the bereaved and help them to find meaning in the way the funeral is celebrated. The minister is faced with those who are still very early in their grief. Being familiar with the early aspects of grief (see chaps. 2 and 3) assists the minister with more of an awareness as to what the bereaved are feeling.

A Liturgy Preparation Sheet (see end of this chapter) is a valuable tool for the grief minister who is meeting with the bereaved, along with *Planning the Catholic Funeral.*

Ministry Toolbox

Please consult the Sample Liturgy Preparation Sheet on page 84.

These resources are invaluable in planning a funeral liturgy (refer to "Recommended Readings" at the end of this book):

Order of Christian Funerals

Planning the Catholic Funeral

Peace Beyond Understanding, Consoling One Another

Sample Liturgy Preparation Sheet

Saint Thomas Aquinas Parish
Nahant, Massachusetts

ORDER OF CHRISTIAN FUNERALS

Liturgy of the Vigil

Time: _____

Place: _____

First Reading _____
Reader: _____
Second Reading _____
Reader: _____

Remembrance _____

Music: _____
(see hymn list)
Other: (photo displays, awards, etc.)
_____
_____
_____
_____
_____

Bereavement Minister:
_____

Life is changed . . . not ended

Saint Thomas Aquinas Parish
Nahant, Massachusetts

Funeral Mass

Pall bearers
_____
_____
_____
_____
Pall _____

First Reading
_____

Reader
_____

Second Reading
_____

Reader
_____

Prayer of Faithful Reader
_____

Special remembrance of other relatives
_____

Presentation of gifts:
_____

Special Remembrances / Remembrance:
_____
_____

Music selections (see list):
_____
_____

Grief Minister as
Compassionate Listener

The Lord is good to all,
and his compassion is over all that he has made. (Ps 145:9)

This final chapter is devoted to the grief minister's role as a compassionate listener. Throughout this book we have explored how we are present to the bereaved in a variety of ministerial roles. In this chapter we will explore how we can effectively be present to the bereaved by being compassionate listeners and mirroring the Lord's compassion. This role is woven through all of the many ways we have experienced the ministry of consolation.

The consoling ministry has a basic theme—that of being a person dedicated to being present to the bereaved. This presence is always active, never passive. In many ways in which ministry occurs it is essential that we be there for the bereaved when needed. Actively listening allows those who are grieving to find in the grief minister one who is compassionate and caring about how they feel during the shattering experience of intense grief. Active listening means the minister not only hears what is being said, but that he or she listens for both nuances and what may be missing. As active listeners we reflect back to the speakers what they have said while gently nudging them into a more spiritual approach. Consider the following dialogue between our minister, Mary, and a bereaved widow:

Widow: "I need to clean the house now that the funeral is over."

Mary: "What do you think Bill (the deceased) would want you to do with his clothing?" "Do you have a favorite charity you would like to donate to?"

People need direction. They often just do not know what to do.

Stress-Filled Time

Experiencing a significant loss is a very troubling time. Often the bereaved feel disoriented and confused. This is especially evident with sudden loss and unexpected losses. Disasters, accidents, terrorism, and other events shock us beyond belief. To accept the loss means that we need some way of being able to live with it. We need to communicate our emotions of this experience. We need to tell this story over and over again in order to accept that it really happened and in so doing also learn to cope with what we are beginning to accept. In this way we are accommodating our loss. Storytelling does not mean remembering every detail.

On Deaf Ears

It is not uncommon in today's society for people to find it difficult to go through grief. Our society is very secular and does not want to face spiritual eventualities. Society and our network of friends and acquaintances do not always want to face loss. Usually people are supportive but in very limited ways. During the funeral and for a brief time afterwards they are willing to talk about the loss. Once the bereaved begin to repeat and retell their story, the support disappears. The sad reality about our culture is that there is considerable avoidance of topics and conversations about death.

A Compassionate Listener

There are many prerequisites facing the grief minister in accepting this way to minister. There has to be a deep commitment to be willing to spend time with the bereaved person. When the minister schedules an appointment to visit, he or she has to be willing to listen without hurrying the bereaved. Sufficient time has to be given for the bereaved to tell their story. In many ways we lead from behind.

The compassionate listener often acts as a spiritual and an emotional guide for the bereaved. The grief minister has to be familiar with what it means to opt for empathy over sympathy. Our society is very conditioned to being sympathetic. This is evident at the time of a funeral. During the wake a very awkward time for many is when they express "sympathy." Sympathy is a passing and very objective expression. We hear people say the words, "I am sorry for your loss," or they may say, "Please accept our condolences." Both of these remarks, while well intentioned, do not really engage the bereaved.

Grief ministers who want to be with the bereaved have to be empathic. Empathy is when we see ourselves in another's position. The empathic statement is, "It must be very difficult for you." This is by far more engaging. It gives the bereaved permission to make an active response. They may tell us, "I am feeling as if part of me has died" or "This is so painful yet I am beginning to accept this."

Listening is a key for all of the ministry times we have explored in this book. It is the essential backdrop for ministry. Listening means empowering the bereaved to feel that their cries have been heard. So many times they feel that everything is falling on deaf ears.

Sharpening Our Listening Skills

It is necessary to have an active presence with the bereaved. We cannot be passive or detached if we want to be effective listeners. The grief minister has to be willing to explore better ways to hear what the bereaved person is communicating. Developing and sharpening up on listening skills is essential.

The good listener does not just silently observe or act as some sort of a container or receptacle to what is being voiced. This passive receiving of thoughts and emotions could do considerable harm. It may drive the bereaved into the doldrums of confusion and make them feel more isolated. The active listener is one who is able to provide some verbal feedback to the bereaved. This may be accomplished with short statements or summaries of what has been communicated. These verbal and nonverbal cues demonstrate to the speaker that you are listening.

It takes time and formation to give the bereaved verbal feedback. Many parishes and institutions practice role-playing just to acquaint the minister with ways to improve as an active listener. The ability to give feedback relies on the minister's ability to create a mental image or model in one's mind of what is being said. This allows for the minister to be empathic and feel with the bereaved. When we have an awareness of the grieving process and its components, we can better filter what is being felt and communicated by the bereaved. This way of conversing is very significant in hospice care as well. End of earthly life conversations are considerably meaningful.

Healing Ways to Hear

The following steps help in becoming effective listeners. These steps help us keep in mind what is necessary to truly communicate with those who need to converse with us.

1. *Develop a presence.* Physically face the one who is speaking with you.

2. *Be attentive.* Stay focused yet relaxed while you listen.

3. *Create a mental picture.* Try to visualize what is being said to you.

4. *Do not try to fix things.* Allow the story to be told as it is.

5. *Do not try to rescue people.* Don't give your solution to problems.

6. *Allow for silences.* Pauses are meant for people to collect thoughts. Wait for them to gather thoughts.

7. *Try to be empathic.* Try to feel what they are feeling in their story.

8. *Give feedback.* Summarize and acknowledge feelings.

9. *Be aware of bodily expression.* Pay attention to posture, gestures, and other nonverbal indicators of emotions.

10. *Allow time.* Do not rush the bereaved. Set aside sufficient time for them.

Condolence Call

There are people in our society who become invisible. They are invisible as people choose not to hear or see what they are really all about. We find this very often with the mentally challenged, the physically challenged, those suffering from terminal illness such as AIDS, victims of domestic violence, and those who are suffering from grief. Our concern is with how we can improve our ability to see and listen to people in more compassionate ways. As grief ministers, we need to instruct our parish communities about the needs facing those who are experiencing loss in their lives. The following phone conversation illustrates the need to fine-tune our listening skills when communicating with the bereaved. Are they in need of ministry? Do they need a condolence call from the grief minister?

Pastoral Scenario

Marian was just recently widowed. She is seventy-two years old and enjoyed forty-three years of marriage. She had the following conversation on the phone with a parish grief minister (G.M.):

Marian: "Hello, I would like to arrange a month's mind Mass for my late husband Charles S."

G.M.: "Oh, yes, Mrs. S. I recall talking with you at the funeral. I hope you are doing well."

Marian: (pause) "It's getting worse rather than better."

G.M.: "I am sorry to hear that. It is still so very early and it must be difficult for you."

Marian: "I feel so alone and sometimes I think he'll come in the door any minute."

G.M.: "We have some fine people who visit people who have had recent losses. Would you like to hear from someone soon?"

Marian: "Oh, thank you. I would like to receive a visit. It is so lonely and quiet here."

Listening Points

When we are with the bereaved, we have to be aware of what to listen for in their conversations. Listening points are times that strike us as a need facing the bereaved. In this previous pastoral scenario, there are a variety of points. We note them from the beginning when Marian mentions how things are getting worse, a point is made. Marian is now moving away from being numbed by the loss and into a time where reality is setting in for her. As this brief conversation continues we hear her cry of an isolated person. She now finds herself alone after the funeral. She's asking for consolation by calling about the memorial Mass. Marian's acceptance of having someone visit her is another point in the conversation that must be heard.

The more familiar we are with the needs facing the bereaved, the better we can minister. The grief minister brings consolation by listening as a person trained to hear in light of an awareness as to what people are going through while they grieve.

Developing Listening Skills

Becoming a good compassionate listener is an ongoing process. We have to be aware of techniques that are useful not only with the bereaved but with others as well. If we are good listeners in our lives, it will translate into a skill that we know is valuable for the grief stricken. Some of the following points will make us more effective. Remember we need to practice these techniques with others.

1. *Stay focused*. We need to be attentive and not suffer distractions such as watching television or listening to the radio or glancing at a magazine.

2. *Allow the person to speak.* The whole idea of listening is defeated when we interrupt a person. Bodily gestures such as placing our hands over our mouth or our chin in our hands can remind us to be quiet.

3. *Avoid being judgmental.* Being defensive and looking for what is right or wrong will not enhance listening.

4. *Avoid negative nonverbal signals.* There are nonverbal indicators you may make such as shrugging your shoulders, using a different tone of voice, looking away from someone, losing eye contact, rolling your eyes, or other gestures that are statements in themselves even when they are partially expressed.

5. *Avoid advice.* Eventually you may be asked to give advice. Do not offer it initially unless asked to do so.

You may and probably will come up with some more ideas about techniques and listening skills. Allowing them to speak and feel heard is compassionate listening.

This chapter is a fitting conclusion for this book. It highlights the importance of the consoling ministry to give voice to those who are trying to express themselves while they grieve. In retrospect, it should be evident that this chapter has been an underlying theme for the multifaceted ministry of consoling. The grief minister who is an empathic listener is the one who can be a healing instrument for so many. Our hopeful prayer is that all of us will progress in better ways to constantly improve the gifts given to us as grief ministers to help those who are grieving.

Ministry Toolbox

Remember the importance of scheduling condolence calls. Practice your listening skills for the pastoral visit.

Do not underestimate the power of a compassionate listener.

Keep in mind the spiritual rewards in consoling the grief stricken.

Notes

Chapter One

1. *Order of Christian Funerals*, General Introduction, par. 8 (Washington, DC: ICEL, 1989).

2. Terence P. Curley, *Console One Another: A Guide for Christian Funerals* (Kansas City, MO: Sheed and Ward, 1993), 72.

3. Ibid. (chap. 2: The Ritual's Symbols for Support), 13.

4. Curley, *Planning the Catholic Funeral* (Collegeville, MN: Liturgical Press, 2005).

5. Curley, *Healing the Broken-Hearted: Consoling the Grief-Stricken* (New York: Alba House, 1995), see chap. 3: Initiating a Parish Bereavement Committee.

Chapter Three

1. Gerald G. May, *Care of Mind, Care of Spirit: A Psychiatrist Explores Spiritual Direction* (San Francisco: HarperSanFrancisco, 1992), 8.

2. Carolyn Gratton, *The Art of Spiritual Guidance* (New York: Crossroad, 1992), 138–39.

3. Curley, *Console One Another*, see schemata of funeral journey, appendix C, 91.

4. Henri Nouwen, *The Inner Voice of Love: A Journey Through Anguish to Freedom* (New York: Doubleday, 1996), 30.

5. Curley, *Six Steps for Managing Loss: A Catholic Guide Through Grief* (New York: Alba House, 1997), 4–11 (Steps adapted to Grief).

Chapter Four

1. Dennis Klass, Phyllis R. Silverman, and Steven L. Nickman, eds., *Continuing Bonds: New Understandings of Grief* (Washington, DC: Taylor & Francis, 1996), xviii.

2. Curley, *The Ministry of Consolation: A Parish Guide for Comforting the Bereaved* (New York: Alba House, 1993), see chap. 3: "Grief Through the Eyes of a Child."

3. Claudia L. Jewett, *Helping Children Cope with Separation and Loss* (Boston: Harvard Common Press, 1982), 8–9.

4. Curley, *The Ministry of Consolation*, 14–15 (Prayer Service Outline for Children).

5. Curley, *Console One Another.*

6. Michael R. Leming and George E. Dickinson, *Understanding Dying, Death, and Bereavement* (New York: Holt, Rinehart, and Winston, 1985), 132 (quote by Helen Galen).

7. Barbara F. Meltz, "Helping Children Live Through Loss and Grief," *The Boston Globe* (September, 1993): A-4 (quote by Rabbi Earl Grollman).

8. Mary DeTurris Poust, *Parenting A Grieving Child* (Chicago: Loyola Press, 2002). See chap. 9, "Ways To Remember: Ritual and the Creation of Memories," which contains interview remarks by Terence P. Curley.

Chapter Five

1. Curley, "The Teenager's Experience of Loss," *Pastoral Life* 46, no. 9 (October 1997): 25–31.

2. Curley, "Healing Grief with a Compassionate Listener," *Pastoral Life* 46, no. 4 (April 1997): 13–18.

Chapter Six

1. Curley, *Challenging the Landscape of Loss: Why What We've Been Told about Grief Doesn't Help* (2015), http://www.amazon.com/Challenging-Landscape-Loss-about-doesnt/dp/1503279634.

Chapter Seven

1. Videos on this topic are available on YouTube. Search "Terence Curley."

2. Curley, *Healing the Broken-Hearted*, 62–63 (Anniversary Prayer Service).

3. Bob Deits, *Life After Loss: A Personal Guide Dealing with Death, Divorce, Job Change, and Relocation* (Tucson: Fisher Books, 1988), 146–47.

4. Ibid., 149.

Chapter Eight

1. Curley, *Six Steps for Managing Loss.* A series of Prayer Experiences are offered, 35–48, which identify psalm meditations with grief moments.

2. Henri J. M. Nouwen, *A Letter of Consolation* (San Francisco: HarperSanFrancisco, 1982), 6, 9.

3. Curley, *Six Steps for Managing Loss.* Insights are provided through steps for the journey through grief. These steps outline emotions/spirituality connected with the experience of loss.

Chapter Nine

1. Paul E. Irion, "The Funeral and the Bereaved," in *Resources for Ministry in Death and Dying*, ed. Larry A. Platt and Roger C. Branch, 211 (Nashville: Broadman Press, 1989).

2. See *Order of Christian Funerals* 118 (Gathering in the Presence of the Body).

Recommended Readings

Consoling Ministry

Attig, Thomas. *How We Grieve: Relearning the World.* Rev. ed. New York: Oxford University Press, 2011.

Curley, Terence P. *The Ministry of Consolation: A Parish Guide for Comforting the Bereaved.* New York: Alba House, 1993.

———. *Healing the Broken-Hearted: Consoling the Grief-Stricken.* New York: Alba House, 1995.

———. *Six Steps for Managing Loss: A Catholic Guide Through Grief.* New York: Alba House, 1997.

———. "A Bill of Rights for the Bereaved." *Pastoral Life* 49, no. 1 (January 2000).

Gilmour, Peter, and David A. Lysik. *Now and at the Hour of Our Death.* Rev. ed. Chicago: Liturgy Training Publications, 1996.

Liturgy Preparation

Boadt, Lawrence, Mary Dombeck, and H. Richard Rutherford. *The Rites of Death and Dying,* 1987, National Meeting of the Federation of Diocesan Liturgical Committees. Collegeville, MN: Liturgical Press, 1988.

Catholic Conference of Canadian Bishops. "The Christian Funeral." *National Bulletin on Liturgy* 22, no. 119 (December 1989): 197–257.

Curley, Terence P. "Bringing Order to Funerals." *The Priest* 56, no. 3 (March 2000).

———. "Grief's Changing Landscape: Far-Reaching Effects for the Pastoral Response." *The Priest* (September 2015).

———. "Cremation and Bodily Resurrection." *The Priest* 55, no. 4 (April 1999). (See also chap. 11 in *Peace Beyond Understanding.*)

————. *Healing: Questions and Answers for Those Who Mourn*. New York: Alba House, 2002.

————. "The Order of Christian Funerals: A Better Connection for Pastoral Care." *The Priest* 47, no. 4 (April 1991).

————. *Peace Beyond Understanding: Consoling One Another*. CreateSpace, 2011. http://www.amazon.com/Peace-Beyond-Understanding-Consoling-Another/dp/1453891080.

————. *Planning the Catholic Funeral*. Collegeville, MN: Liturgical Press, 2005.

Order of Christian Funerals. Washington, DC: International Commission on English in the Liturgy (ICEL), 1989.

Order of Christian Funerals, Appendix 2: Cremation. Totowa, NJ: Catholic Book Publishing, 1997.

Rutherford, H. Richard. *The Death of a Christian*. Collegeville, MN: Liturgical Press, 1991.

Spakes, Robert, and Richard Rutherford. "The Order of Christian Funerals: A Study in Bereavement and Lament." *Worship* 60, no. 6 (1986): 499.

Formation and Instruction

Curley, Terence P. *Six Steps for Managing Loss: A Catholic Guide Through Grief*. New York: Alba House, 1997.

————. "Spiritual Steps for Managing Loss." *Pastoral Life* 47, no. 11 (1998).

Francis, Pope. *Misericordiae Vultus*, The Face of Mercy. Papal bull for the holy year 2015–16.

Gratton, Carolyn. *The Art of Spiritual Direction*. New York: Crossroad, 1998.

Nouwen, Henri J. M. *The Inner Voice of Love: A Journey Through Anguish to Freedom*. New York: Doubleday, 1996.

————. "A Letter of Consolation." San Francisco: HarperSanFrancisco, 1982.

The Psalms and Religious Expression

Anderson, Bernhard W. *Out of the Depths: The Psalms Speak for Us Today*. Rev. ed. Louisville, KY: Westminster John Knox, 2000.

Brueggeman, Walter. *The Message of the Psalms: A Theological Commentary*. Minneapolis: Augsburg, 1984.

Craghan, John F. *Psalms for All Seasons*. Rev. ed. Collegeville, MN: Liturgical Press, 2013.

Creach, Jerome F. D. *Psalms*. Interpretation Bible Studies. Louisville, KY: Westminster John Knox, 1998.

Grief Support and Hospice Care

Curley, Terence P. *A Way of the Cross for the Bereaved*. New York: Alba House, 1996.

Nouwen, Henri J. M. *Can You Drink the Cup?* 10th Anniversary ed. Notre Dame, IN: Ave Maria Press, 2006.

O'Rourke, Michelle. *Befriending Death: Henri Nouwen and a Spirituality of Dying*. Maryknoll, NY: Orbis, 2009.

New Psychology of Loss

Bonanno, George A. *The Other Side of Sadness: What the New Science of Bereavement Tells Us about Life after Loss*. New York: Basic Books, 2009.

Curley, Terence P. *Challenging the Landscape of Loss: Why What We've Been Told about Grief Doesn't Help*. Swampscott, MA: Paloma, 2015.

Klass, Dennis, Phyllis R. Silverman, and Steven L. Nickman. *Continuing Bonds: New Understandings of Grief*. Washington, DC: Taylor & Francis, 1996.

Neimeyer, Robert. *Lessons of Loss: A Guide To Coping*. Memphis, TN: Center for the Study of Loss and Transition, 2006.

Silverman, Phyllis R. *Never Too Young To Know: Death in Children's Lives*. New York: Oxford University Press, 2000.

Internet Resources

Search "Terence Curley" on YouTube for videos that address a variety of grief topics.

Go to Fr. Curley's blog at http://manageyourloss.net/ for information on managing grief.

Audiovisual Guides for Good Grief

The following audiovisuals by Fr. Terence Curley are available through St. Paul's Alba House Communications, Canfield, OH, 1-800-533-2522 (all are four-part, half-hour presentations):

From Darkness to Light: A Healing Path Through Grief

Through the Dark Valley: Healing Steps for Managing Loss

Journey to Healing: A Ministry for the Bereaved

Arise and Walk: A Christian Grieving Guide

Rebuilding Trust and Hope: New Models for Grief and Mourning for the New Evangelization

The Bright Promise of Immortality: New Science and Meaning for Grief Ministry

Other Titles by Terence P. Curley